Graphics on the
BBC
Microcomputer

Other books published by Prentice-Hall International

BASIC PROGRAMMING ON THE BBC MICROCOMPUTER,
Neil Cryer and Pat Cryer

THE BBC MICROCOMPUTER FOR BEGINNERS,
Seamus Dunn and Valerie Morgan

100 PROGRAMS FOR THE BBC MICROCOMPUTER,
John Gordon

THE BBC MICROCOMPUTER DISK COMPANION,
Tony Latham

Graphics on the
BBC
Microcomputer

Neil Cryer
Chelsea College, University of London

Pat Cryer
Educational Consultant and Honorary
Research Fellow, University of Surrey

and Andrew Cryer

Prentice/Hall PHI International

ENGLEWOOD CLIFFS, NEW JERSEY   LONDON   NEW DELHI   RIO DE JANEIRO
SINGAPORE   SYDNEY   TOKYO   TORONTO   WELLINGTON

British Library Cataloguing in Publication Data

Cryer, Neil
  Graphics on the BBC micro.
  1. Computer graphics   2. BBC Microcomputer
  I. Title   II. Cryer, Pat
  III. Cryer, Andrew
  001.64'43   T385

  ISBN 0-13-363283-0

Library of Congress Cataloging in Publication Data

Cryer, Neil
  Graphics on the BBC micro.

  Includes index.
  1. Computer graphics. 2. BBC Microcomputer - Programming.
  I. Cryer, Pat. II. Cryer, Andrew. III. Title: Graphics on the BBC micro.
  T385.C78   1983   001.64'43   83-13770
  ISBN 0-13-363283-0 (pbk.)
  ISBN 0-13-363242-3 (cassette)

ISBN 0-13-363283-0

PRENTICE-HALL INTERNATIONAL INC., London
PRENTICE-HALL OF AUSTRALIA PTY., LTD., Sydney
PRENTICE-HALL CANADA, INC., Toronto
PRENTICE-HALL OF INDIA PRIVATE LIMITED, New Delhi
PRENTICE-HALL OF JAPAN, INC., Tokyo
PRENTICE-HALL OF SOUTHEAST ASIA PTE., LTD., Singapore
PRENTICE-HALL INC., Englewood Cliffs, New Jersey
PRENTICE-HALL DO BRASIL LTDA., Rio de Janeiro
WHITEHALL BOOKS LIMITED, Wellington, New Zealand

Printed in Great Britain by A. Wheaton & Co. Ltd., Exeter

10 9 8 7 6 5 4 3 2

Contents

Preface

This is our second book on programming for the BBC Microcomputer and we see it as a natural extension of the first - BASIC Programming on the BBC Microcomputer. That first book was published in the Spring of 1982 and gave a comprehensive introduction to BBC BASIC. In this present book, we show how to capitalise on the superb colour and graphics features, which have made the BBC Microcomputer so widely acclaimed.

We have written this book so that it can be used at any of three levels, for the hobbyist and the professional alike:

At the simplest level, you may just want to scan through to see what can be achieved with colour graphics on the BBC Microcomputer. When you spot an illustration of a screen display that appeals to you, you merely type in the listing, run it and sit back to enjoy the display!

At the next level you may want to produce pictures, shapes, graphs, histograms, pie charts, etc. to display your own data. We have arranged for you to achieve very professional-looking results quite easily. You merely find a screen display that looks suitable and use its listing. Sometimes you can feed in your own data directly, but where you have to edit the listing, we explain how to do it.

The third level is for those who want to learn how to program graphics on the BBC Microcomputer. If you already have some idea of BASIC programming, you will find that the book takes you gently through the various graphics statements, showing when and how to use them.

With this book, it really is possible to achieve professional-looking and dramatic displays of your own design, quickly and easily. This is largely because we have provided routines which you can call on to take care of the rather mundane and irksome parts of programming graphics, such as setting up and scaling the displays. We explain how to use these routines and we list them fully in an appendix. Another appendix explains how they work and the techniques on which they rely.

These routines are also available, with the other programs in the book, for purchase on cassette tape. Not only does this free you from having to type them into the computer; it also means no typing errors. So it is a major advantage.

With this book, we welcome Andrew Cryer to the family team. His contribution to programming has been invaluable and we have appreciated his support and constructive criticism on other aspects of the writing.

We would like to thank those people whose names do not appear on the front cover but who contributed significantly to the production of this book. In particular Tony Brain of Chelsea College and Roger Wilson of Acorn Computers Ltd both made exceptionally valuable comments on early drafts of the manuscript. Our editor, Giles Wright of Prentice Hall International has been a constant source of support, encouragement and efficiency throughout the entire writing process. We are also grateful to Wendy Cryer for her drawings of the 'professor'. The self-study aspects of the book have benefited much from the association of one of us (Pat Cryer) with the education branch of a multi-national computing concern and with the Institute of Educational Development at the University of Surrey.

Neil Cryer   Pat Cryer

Andrew Cryer

London
September 1983

Graphics on the
BBC
Microcomputer

0 Introduction

0.0 About this book

This book enters the fascinating area of computer graphics! It is written with special reference to the BBC Microcomputer and it teaches how to use the BBC Microcomputer to produce such displays as pictures, shapes, graphs, histograms, pie charts, etc. Yet the book is much more than a teaching book. We have written it assuming that you may want to use it for any of the following three reasons, and we have made provision for all three.

i. You may want to see what the BBC Microcomputer can do in the way of colour graphics, and not want to develop a graphics display for any specific purpose. If so, since the displays are

1

opposite or next to the programs which produce them, you can simply choose the display you like, type in the program and run it to get an identical display.

ii. You may be looking for a graphics display to help you with a particular job or problem. If so, you simply flip through the book to find the display which most nearly suits your purposes. Then you read our hints and advice on how to modify it.

iii. You may want to make your own graphics programs. With this in mind, we describe and explain the necessary BBC BASIC instructions and show how to use them. We also provide various routines to save you time when you program sophisticated graphics displays, and we show you how to use them.

In iii. we mentioned routines to save you time when you program graphics displays. Let us explain. Whenever you program graphics, you will find that you keep needing routines to do certain jobs, like scaling data so that the display fits the screen, or like drawing and graduating axes of a graph. We do not just teach you how to program these for yourself. We actually supply them as procedures for you! They are listed in Appendix 1 for you to type in and save, although you can also buy them ready-recorded on cassette tape. You merely call on the procedure which you happen to want for a particular job, without having to program it yourself. You do not even have to understand how it works - although we do explain in Appendix 2. So, in effect, these routines extend BBC BASIC! They enormously simplify your graphics programming, so that you can immediately get on with the exciting tasks of producing your own unique displays.

You will get the most out of this book if you have a BBC Microcomputer and a colour television or monitor. This is for two reasons. Firstly, the BBC Microcomputer is particularly renowned for its colour graphics facilities, and this book exploits them to the full. Secondly, the book presents the material in such a way that you will learn by doing, as well as by reading. We assume that you are sitting at or near the computer as you read, and will want to break every few minutes to try some of the activities which we suggest.

We also assume that you are already familiar with the essentials of programming in BBC BASIC. If you are not, you should first work through our previous book BASIC Programming on the BBC Microcomputer, which is also published by Prentice Hall.

In this book, our way of working is to give you some information, and then to follow it with an Activities section, in which we ask you to do something for yourself to consolidate. Consequently you learn by doing. We now continue this chapter with a few short sections to illustrate this way of working. First we give information. We tell you about the BBC Microcomputer, as a computer for programming graphics and then we explain how to save, load and join programs. We think it is important for you to become proficient at this quite early on. Although we do not specifically ask you to do it until some way into the book, we are quite sure that you will want to save, load and join the routines that you develop yourself as you go through the book. Afterwards we give a short section of Activities where you might like to do something yourself.

0.1 The two models of the BBC Microcomputer

The BBC Microcomputer is available in two models, Model A and Model B. The memory of the Model B is greater than that of Model A (32K of RAM compared with 16K). You can upgrade a Model A by adding more memory. This makes it equivalent to a Model B for all programming purposes.

The greater memory of the Model B gives the advantages of a larger number of display modes, a greater choice of colour and more detail (resolution) on the screen. Also, as graphics programs tend to be rather long, especially when they call on a number of our graphics procedures, a Model A may run out of memory. A further advantage of Model B is concerned with saving and retrieving programs. Both models allow you to save and retrieve using cassette tape and an ordinary tape recorder, but Model B allows you to add a disk system. The disk drives are not cheap but they give speed and reliability.

We have not lost sight of the fact that you may be using a Model A for your graphics programming. Although you will not have as many facilities as Model B owners, you do, nevertheless, have sufficient to make it worthwhile to program graphics. In particular we provide some very useful routines which allow most of the graphics to operate in the Teletext mode, mode 7. This offers the full range of colours and requires only 1K of memory! With a Model B and with long programs which require a large amount of memory for data storage, you will also find these routines valuable. In Appendix 2 we explain how to estimate whether or not a program will fit into the memory of your model of computer, depending on which of our procedures it calls.

0.2 Loading, saving and joining programs

In this section, we explain how to save, load and join programs. As we mentioned earlier, we expect that you will want to become proficient at this in order to save, load and join routines that you develop yourself as a result of working through this book.

There is another reason why you will want to save, load and join programs. As we also mentioned, a feature of this book is that we provide various routines to do those jobs which you are likely to keep needing for programming graphics. After the first few chapters, we repeatedly refer to these routines throughout the text and we supply them as procedures, listed in Appendix 1. To use them, you will either have to buy the cassette on which they are ready-recorded, or you will have to type them into your computer and save them, ready to join them to your existing program.

We have adopted the approach of saving all of our routines in what is called the *EXEC format, and we advise you to do the same. Using this format, the routines can be retrieved from tape or disk, just as if you had typed them in from the keyboard. Since the lines of our routines have numbers over 9000, they will not overwrite your existing program. They simply join onto whatever program is already in memory. This is in contrast to loading using the LOAD command, which irretrievably removes all trace of any previous program.

To save any program on tape in the *EXEC format, first type the following where NAME may be up to ten characters long:

*SPOOL "NAME"

Enter this by pressing RETURN.

The computer responds with the following message:

RECORD then RETURN

So set the tape recorder to record and then press the RETURN key. The prompt and flashing cursor appear.

Next enter:

LIST

This causes the program listing to appear on the screen. It also sends the listing to a buffer inside the computer, ready for recording onto the tape.

When the listing is complete, enter:

    *SPOOL

This completes the saving process and sends any remaining program from the buffer to the tape recorder.

To load anything which has been saved in the *EXEC format, rewind the tape, and then simply type the following and set the tape recorder to play:

    *EXEC "NAME"

Once you have pressed RETURN, you will see the lines of the program appearing very rapidly on the screen, just as if a phantom typist were typing them. Any program already in the computer is unaffected, as long as it does not have the same line numbers. Then the incoming lines would overwrite the existing ones, just as if you were typing them in yourself.

If you have a disk system, you will clearly want to transfer the programs to disk - but you will have to be more careful in choosing names because a name can only be up to seven characters long. The cassette tape available with this book can be read into a BBC Microcomputer with the disk operating system, by first switching to the tape file system by issuing the command:

    *TAPE

Programs and procedures, etc. can then be loaded as already described. Once the program lines are in the computer, the following command switches back to the disk file system, ready for saving:

    *DISK

For complete programs, it is more usual to save and reload using the following commands, respectively:

    SAVE "NAME"

and

    LOAD "NAME"

Using LOAD and SAVE is much faster than using *EXEC and *SPOOL.

0.3 Activities

These activities illustrate the saving and joining of programs using
*SPOOL and *EXEC.

i. Start by entering the following two lines of program so that
you have something to save:

        10 PROCtrial
        20 END

ii. Now save these lines under the name MAIN-PROG using the
*SPOOL command, as described in the previous section.

iii. Enter NEW. This is to remove these lines from memory and
so convince you, when you see them again, that you have really
retrieved them from tape.

iv. Now, using the *SPOOL command, save the following lines
under the name TRIAL. They define the procedure PROCtrial
which was called in line 10 of the MAIN-PROG:

        100 DEF PROCtrial
        110 PRINT "This is proc trial"
        120 ENDPROC

v. You should now have two blocks of data saved: under the
names MAIN-PROG and TRIAL. Enter NEW to clear the existing
lines of procedure and then retrieve MAIN-PROG using the
*EXEC command. You will have to wind the tape back to the
start and set the tape recorder to play. You will now see the
lines of the first program rapidly typed up on the screen
preceded by the message:

        >>LIST

        Syntax error

and followed by the message:

        >>*SPOOL

        Syntax error
        >

We discuss these error messages in Section 0.4.

vi. List the program lines recovered so far. This should confirm that only the first set of lines, up to line 20 have reappeared. Try entering RUN. Does this produce the following error message?

No such FN/PROC at line 10

vii. Now similarly retrieve "TRIAL" using the *EXEC command. Do the set of lines which define the procedure appear?

viii. Enter LIST to confirm that the two sets of lines have been joined to give a complete program. Does the program run now?

_____

0.4 Discussion of activities

Activity 0.3 v: You may ignore the Syntax error messages. They always arise at the start and end of loading of a program using *SPOOL, and arise because the > sign which precedes the *SPOOL is a mechanism by which the system is prevented from responding to recorded commands.

1 Fundamentals of graphics

1.0 Introduction

This chapter is about plotting points and drawing lines and curves. It teaches you how to use the graphics instructions which are available within BBC BASIC, and we have called it 'fundamentals of graphics'. This is to distinguish it from the more sophisticated graphics of later chapters, which rely, not only on the instructions available within BBC BASIC, but also on procedures which we provide for you.

1.1 The display modes of a Model B BBC Microcomputer

The BBC Microcomputer allows you to make up a display using the following:

- Teletext characters which you will have seen on television's Ceefax and Oracle;
- alpha numeric characters, i.e. letters and numbers of the sort used in ordinary text; and
- rectangular spots, which can make up lines and shapes.

Model B of the BBC Microcomputer offers eight display modes, allowing a choice of character size and spot size. These modes are numbered from 0 to 7.

Mode 7 is the mode in which the computer first turns on. It can display both text characters and graphics in eight colours. 40 characters can be fitted on a line with 25 lines per screen. The mode is sometimes called the Teletext mode as it allows the colours and symbols of television's Teletext. Teletext colours and graphics have to be turned on and off in a completely different way from that for all the other seven modes. Mode 7 requires 1K of memory, which is far less than for any other mode, and this offers advantages that make it worthwhile to program Teletext graphics. Nevertheless mode 7 is not really a true graphics mode - and we consider it separately later (see Chapter 15). Modes 3 and 6 are not graphics modes either because they allow only text characters.

We shall be concentrating on the other five modes, the 'graphics modes', namely modes 0,1,2,4 and 5. Briefly their characteristics are as follows:

Mode 0 allows the display of 640 by 256 graphics spots in two colours. In addition any text comes out with 80 characters to a line with 32 lines on the screen. Mode 0 requires 20K of memory, which is the maximum for any display.

Mode 1 allows the display of 320 by 256 graphics spots each of which may be in any of four colours. Text comes out with 40 characters to the line with 32 lines on the screen. Mode 1 requires 20K of memory.

Mode 2 allows the display of 160 by 256 graphics spots each of which may be in any of the 8 available colours, which may be steady or flashing. Text comes out with 20 characters to the line with 32 lines on the screen. Mode 2 requires 20K of memory.

Mode 4 allows the display of 320 by 256 graphics spots, each in one of two colours. Text comes out with 40 characters to the line with 32 lines on the screen. Mode 4 requires 10K of memory.

Mode 5 allows the display of 160 by 256 graphics spots each of which may be in any of four colours. Text comes out with 20 characters to the line with 32 lines on the screen. Mode 5 requires 10K of memory.

In those modes which allow a greater number of spots, the spots are accordingly smaller. This means that these graphics displays can show more detail, which is described by saying that there is a greater 'resolution'.

Table 1.1 gives a summary of the facilities in the various modes.

mode	7	6	5	4	3	2	1	0
characters per line	40	40	20	40	80	20	40	80
lines per screen	25	25	32	32	25	32	32	32
spots horizontally	-	-	160	320	-	160	320	640
spots vertically	-	-	256	256	-	256	256	256
memory required	1	8	10	10	16	20	20	20
colours available	Teletext features	2	4	2	2	8+8	4	2

Table 1.1 Features available in various modes

1.2 Graphics on a Model A BBC Microcomputer

Model A of the BBC Microcomputer is limited in the amount of memory available and so you will need to add to it if you want sophisticated graphics. This is particularly so because, if memory is being used for the display, it is not available for program storage. So there may be times when there is a clash between the memory requirements of a long program and a complex graphics display. For this reason many people add extra chips to make the Model A equivalent to the Model B in terms of memory. The Model A Microcomputer can only produce displays in modes 4, 5, 6 and 7. This means that the graphics is limited to four colours with 160 by 256 spots or two colours with 320 by 256 spots.

Many of the programs in this book will run on the Model A, but a few are too long to fit into the limited memory and have to be run on either an expanded Model A or the full Model B. These are equivalent, as far as length of program is concerned.

1.3 Getting into a mode

When you turn on the BBC Microcomputer, you are in mode 7. You can select another mode, say mode 4, by entering one of the following. Either is acceptable because although BBC BASIC does not require a space in front of a number, it normally allows one to make the reading easier.

        MODE 4

or

        MODE4

This statement causes the screen to clear, and anything that you now write is in the new mode.

1.4 Addressing pixels

In the graphics modes (0, 1, 2, 4 and 5) you may draw pictures, shapes and graphs by lighting up rectangular spots on the screen. Each spot is very small and is called a 'pixel'. The size and shape of a pixel varies according to the graphics mode, as shown in Figures 1.1a,b,c.

*Figure 1.1a. The relative size and shape of a pixel
in mode 0.*

*Figure 1.1b. The relative size and shape of a pixel
in mode 1.*

*Figure 1.1c. The relative size and shape of a pixel
in mode 2.*

Theoretically BBC BASIC takes the smallest available pixel to
be so tiny that 1280 would fit onto the screen horizontally and
1024 would fit onto the screen vertically. Unfortunately, though,
present models of the BBC Microcomputer give rather larger pixels.
Even in mode 0, a maximum of only half this number fit onto the
screen horizontally and only a quarter vertically. Nevertheless,
irrespective of mode, you always have to address the screen as if
it had the theoretical resolution, i.e. as if it had 1280 pixels in the
horizontal direction and 1024 vertically. These theoretical pixels are
called 'addressable points'.

The position of an addressable point has to be specified by how
far across from the left it is - which is called its 'X co-ordinate' -
and how far up it is - which is called its 'Y co-ordinate'. Thus the
co-ordinate of a position at the bottom left-hand corner of the
screen is 0,0. This is illustrated in Figure 1.2 which shows the
co-ordinates of various points on the screen. For example, the
co-ordinates of a point half way across the bottom of the screen
are 640,0 and the co-ordinates of the centre of the screen are
640,512.

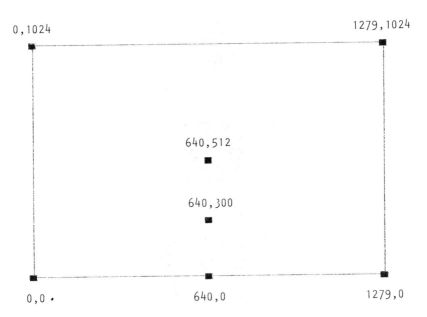

Figure 1.2. The co-ordinates of various points on the screen.

Figure 1.3a shows the pixels in the letter M in mode 0. There are several addressable points per pixel. Figure 1.3b shows an enlargement of the four pixels in the lower left-hand corner of Figure 1.3a with the addressable points in the first pixel marked off and labelled. To simplify things, BBC BASIC requires that, to address a pixel, you merely have to address one of the addressable points within it. Any one will do. It is rather as if you were writing to a firm which had taken over and spread into a number of neighbouring premises. It would not matter which one you addressed, as the firm would be reached via any one of them. To carry the analogy further, it would be pointless to go to more than one. It is equally pointless to address more than one addressable point within a pixel. One is enough and any one will do. We shall illustrate by looking at each mode separately.

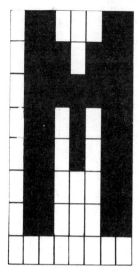

Figure 1.3a. The pixels within the letter M in mode 0.

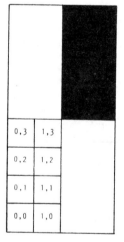

Figure 1.3b. An enlargement of the four pixels in the lower left-hand corner of Figure 1.3a. Addressable points in the first pixel are marked off and labelled, assuming that the M is at the lower left-hand corner of the screen.

In mode 0 there are 640 by 256 pixels. As there are always 1280 by 1024 addressable points, a pixel consists of an area two addressable points wide and four addressable points high. As you see in Figure 1.3b, the first pixel at the extreme left-hand corner of the screen contains the following addressable points:

0,3	1,3
0,2	1,2
0,1	1,1
0,0	1,0

You can of course address the whole pixel via any one of these points. In any mode the pixel corresponds to the smallest point of light on the screen.

In modes 1 and 4 there are 320 by 256 pixels, each consisting of sixteen addressable points, four horizontally and four vertically. In modes 2 and 5 there are 160 by 256 pixels, each consisting of thirty-two addressable points, eight horizontally and four vertically.

1.5 Activities

i. Enter the program given in Listing 1.1. (You will find it over the page, with the corresponding screen displays: Screen Display 1.1a, 1.1b and 1.1c.) This program writes 1234 on the bottom left-hand corner of the screen and then enlarges this by sixteen times. The size of the original characters and of the enlargement depends on the display mode chosen. It does not matter if you do not understand all the lines in the procedure definition of the program, because we merely want to demonstrate the different sizes of the pixels in various modes.

ii. Run the program several times and, each time, when the program asks you to choose a mode, choose a different one from the graphics modes 0, 1, 2, 4 or 5. (You can see which ones we chose in order to get our displays, because we show the dialogues between a user and the computer, and we underline the data that the user feeds in.) Can you see why the same program gives different sizes of enlarged characters in modes 0, 1 and 5 even though the screen is addressed identically in each? We discuss the reason in Section 1.10 at the end of the chapter.

This program illustrates how the size
of characters depends on mode.

When you are asked for a mode, please
enter 0, 1, 2, 4 or 5.

Which mode?0

Mode: 0

1234

Screen Display 1.1a

This program illustrates how the size
of characters depends on mode.

When you are asked for a mode, please
enter 0, 1, 2, 4 or 5.

Which mode?1

Mode: 1

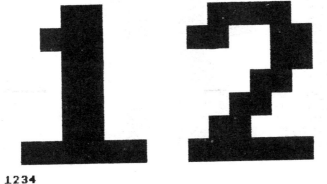

1234

Screen Display 1.1b

This program illustrates how the size
of characters depends on mode.

When you are asked for a mode, please
enter 0, 1, 2, 4 or 5.

Which mode?5

Screen Display 1.1c

```
      Listing 1.1
10 MODE4
20 PRINT '  '  '  '  "This program illustrates how the
   size"
30 PRINT '  '  "of characters depends on mode."
40 PRINT '  '  "When you are asked for a mode, please"
50 REPEAT
60    INPUT '  '  "enter 0, 1, 2, 4 or 5."  '  '  '  "Which
      mode",mode
70    UNTIL (mode>=0 AND mode<6) AND mode<>3
80 MODE mode
90 PRINT TAB(0,5);"Mode: ";mode
100 PRINT TAB(0,31);"1234";
110 FOR X=0 TO 63
120    FOR Y=0 TO 31
130       IF POINT(X,Y)<>0 THEN PROCpixel(X,Y)
140       NEXT Y
150    NEXT X
160 END
170 :
180 DEF PROCpixel(X,Y)
190 Mag=20
200 XCOR=X*Mag
210 YCOR=Y*Mag
220 MOVE XCOR-Mag/2,YCOR-Mag/2
230 MOVE XCOR+Mag/2,YCOR-Mag/2
240 PLOT 85,XCOR-Mag/2,YCOR+Mag/2
250 PLOT 85,XCOR+Mag/2,YCOR+Mag/2
260 ENDPROC
```

1.6 Drawing lines

The MOVE and DRAW statements are elementary statements for
computer graphics. DRAW draws a straight line from the last
point addressed on the screen to a point whose co-ordinates have
to be supplied with the statement. Thus a program line such as
the following draws a straight line to the centre of the screen,
point 640,512, from wherever the last graphics statement finished
off:

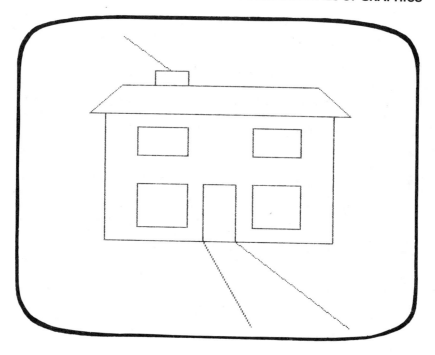

Screen Display 1.2

        120 DRAW 640,512

MOVE is a statement which sets the starting position for a DRAW and other graphics statements. By itself, it produces no visible effect on the screen. By way of example, the following is a simple program in graphics mode 4 to draw a line between the point 10,0 and the point 640,1024 which is half way across the top of the screen.

        10 MODE 4
        20 MOVE 10,0
        30 DRAW 640,1024
        40 END

Line 20 produces no visible action but specifies the starting point for the DRAW in line 30.

```
Listing 1.2
10 MODE 4
20 REM A picture-drawing program.
30 REM The picture is made mainly
40 REM from rectangular blocks. The
50 REM data is in the form of the
60 REM x,y co-ordinates of the lower
70 REM left-hand side, width, height.
80 REPEAT
90    READ X,Y,W,H
100   PROCbox(X,Y,W,H)
110   UNTIL X=-1
120
130 REM Now the other lines
140 MOVE 100,750 :DRAW 200,850
150 DRAW 800,850 :DRAW 900,750
160 DRAW 100,750
170 MOVE 350,900 :DRAW 200,1024
180 MOVE 450,300 :DRAW 600,0
190 MOVE 550,300 :DRAW 900,0
200 END
210
220 DEF PROCbox(X,Y,W,H)
230 MOVE X,Y :DRAW X+W,Y :DRAW X+W,Y+H
240 DRAW X,Y+H :DRAW X,Y
250 ENDPROC
260
270 DATA 300,850,100,50 :REM chimney
280 DATA 150,300,700,450 :REM house
290 REM Now windows and door
300 DATA 250,350,150,150,600,350,150,150
310 DATA 250,600,150,100,600,600,150,100
320 DATA 450,300,100,200
330 DATA -1,-1,-1,-1
```

The following is an additional program line which draws a second line from where the previous line stopped at the top of the screen, down to the bottom right-hand corner 1280,0:

```
35 DRAW 1280,0
```

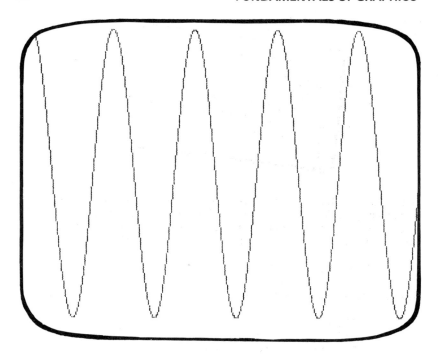

Screen Display 1.3

Consequently, the following program would draw a rectangle, the four lines containing the DRAW statements produce the four sides:

```
10 MODE 4
20 MOVE 50,50
30 DRAW 1000,50
40 DRAW 1000,1000
50 DRAW 50,1000
60 DRAW 50,50
70 END
```

We will now show you a general purpose program to draw any shape that can be made from a series of rectangles. In this program we have a need to draw many rectangles and so it is convenient to enclose a set of lines, similar to the above, in a

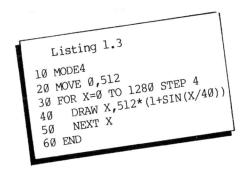

```
Listing 1.3

10 MODE4
20 MOVE 0,512
30 FOR X=0 TO 1280 STEP 4
40    DRAW X,512*(1+SIN(X/40))
50    NEXT X
60 END
```

procedure. Then each rectangle is drawn by a call to this procedure, as for example in the following program line, where X and Y are the co-ordinates of the bottom left-hand corner and W and H are respectively the width and height of the box:

    30 PROCbox(X,Y,W,H)

The procedure to draw the box is defined by the following lines:

    220 DEF PROCbox(X,Y,W,H)
    230 MOVE X,Y :DRAW X+W,Y :DRAW X+W,Y+H
    240 DRAW X,Y+H :DRAW X,Y
    250 ENDPROC

In our program the values of X, Y, W and H are stored in DATA statements for each of the rectangles which make up the major part of the display.

Such a program can be written to draw a variety of shapes. Ours draws a house, which is shown in Screen Display 1.2. A few extra DRAW statements have been included to draw in the few sections of the house, such as the roof, which are not rectangular. The complete program is given in Listing 1.2.

1.7 Activities

---

i. Run the picture-drawing program of Listing 1.2.

ii. Construct your own set of data for drawing some other shape, and run the program to test it.

1.8 Drawing simple curves

You can use the MOVE and DRAW statements to draw simple curves. We illustrate this with a program to draw a wave. For obtaining alternating values, we rely on the mathematical function SIN(X). As X increases in magnitude, the function gives values which alternate between -1 and +1. To get a screen display following the same shape, we make the position across the screen correspond to X and the height up the screen correspond to 1+SIN(X). Multiplying by 512 makes sure that the values representing co-ordinates up the screen run from 0 to 1024 instead of from 0 to +2. Dividing X by 40 reduces the number of oscillations to make the display fit better onto the screen. 512*(1+SIN(X/40)) gives values varying from 0 to 1024, suitable for addressing the height of the screen in screen co-ordinates. The complete program for drawing the wave is in Listing 1.3, opposite the corresponding screen display, Screen Display 1.3.

1.9 Activities

---

i. Run the curve-drawing program of Listing 1.3.

ii. Can you work out what would happen if you had left out the MOVE statement in line 20? Try it to see.

iii. Try the effect of adding STEP 4 to line 30. We comment in Section 1.10.

iv. Try to adapt the program to draw some other curve.

1.10 Discussion of activities

Activity 1.5: The characters are printed in different sizes in modes 0, 1 and 5, because the pixels are of different sizes in these modes (see Figure 1.1 a,b,c).

Activity 1.9 iii: With drawing curves, there is always a compromise between speed and smoothness. The STEP 4 speeds up the display, but the appearance is coarser.

2 Colouring displays

2.0 Introduction

Colour livens up any graphics display! It makes the display more attractive and it adds meaning by making features stand out. The BBC Microcomputer is particularly renowned for its colour graphics, and this chapter shows how to make full use of them. You will of course find it best to have a colour television or monitor, but even with a black and white one, displays should be improved by being in various shades of grey, rather than just black and white.

2.1 Available colours

The BBC Microcomputer is often said to offer a maximum of sixteen colours. This is not strictly true. Actually only eight colours are available, but they can be either flashing or non-flashing - which gives sixteen options. Table 2.1 lists what we call their 'absolute colour numbers'. We describe these numbers as absolute because they cannot be changed. They are always the same irrespective of the mode. This is in contrast to the colour numbers which appear in the various statements that set colour, where you can set the colour given by a particular number. Although it may seem confusing to have two sets of colour numbers, redefining colours does allow some very attractive and sophisticated graphics programming, which we discuss in Chapter 5.

0 = black	8 = flashing black/white
1 = red	9 = flashing red/cyan
2 = green	10 = flashing green/magenta
3 = yellow	11 = flashing yellow/blue
4 = blue	12 = flashing blue/yellow
5 = magenta	13 = flashing magenta/green
6 = cyan	14 = flashing cyan/red
7 = white	15 = flashing white/black

Table 2.1 The absolute colour numbers

In this chapter we deal with default colour numbers, i.e. with colour numbers as they are if you take no steps to redefine them. The default colour associated with any colour number depends on the mode - which is of course not true of an absolute colour. For example, in modes 0 and 4, which are the so-called two colour modes, the default colour numbers represent the following colours:

        colour 0 = black
        colour 1 = white

Whereas in modes 1 and 5 the default colour numbers represent the following colours:

        colour 0 = black
        colour 1 = red
        colour 2 = yellow
        colour 3 = white

The full range of sixteen colours is available only in mode 2, where the colour numbers are initially set equal to the absolute colour number.

2.2 Setting foreground and background colour for text

When setting the colour of graphics displays, BBC BASIC requires you to distinguish between foreground and background colours. There can be only one background colour, but there can be as many foreground colours as you wish to program - provided of course that you are in a mode which allows that many colours. The statement for setting text colour is COLOUR, followed by the colour number.

For the foreground the colour is merely as given above, for the particular mode. For the background, however, the colour number is obtained by adding 128 to the normal colour numbers. By way of illustration, the following three lines of program set 5 as the graphics mode, yellow as the foregound colour and red as the background colour of any text to follow:

```
10 MODE 5
20 COLOUR 2   :REM foreground = yellow
30 COLOUR 129 :REM background = red
40 CLS
```

Line 10 sets the mode and, in so doing, clears the screen to black and resets all the colours to their default values. Lines 20 and 30 set up new values for the foreground and background colours but only for any future writing to the screen. In line 40 the statement CLS - meaning 'clear screen' - clears the screen to the background colour of red.

2.3 Activities

Enter each of the following commands in the direct mode and note the colours that you get on the screen, particularly the foreground colour (the colour of the writing) and the background colour.

```
MODE 5
COLOUR 1
COLOUR 2
```

```
COLOUR 3
COLOUR 129
COLOUR 130
COLOUR 0
COLOUR 131
hello
```

Have the table of colours for mode 5 alongside you and make sure that you can explain the colours of each of the lines of writing, both foreground and background. Do you see that the colour numbers affect only the writing which follows? They leave previous writing unaltered.

2.4 Setting foreground and background colours for graphics

The GCOL statement sets the colour for graphics - or, to be more precise, one form of the GCOL statement sets the colour for graphics. This form is GCOL 0,C and we will not mention the other forms yet. The GCOL 0,C form is the graphics equivalent of the COLOUR statement, in that it controls both the foreground and background colours and affects the colour of the graphics operations that follow its execution. C is the colour number - but you should bear in mind that the GCOL statement, like the other statements for colour, takes the redefinable colour, not the absolute colour.

Provided C has a value between 0 and 15 (depending on mode), it sets foreground i.e. the colour of what you draw on the screen.

To set the background colour, obtain a value for C by adding 128 to the number of the colour that you want. Again, the range of values available depends on the mode. Next use GCOL 0,C. Then, when you clear the screen using the statement CLG, which stands for 'Clear Graphics', the background colour changes accordingly. For example, setting the screen to red for either of the four-colour modes would require the following lines:

```
10 MODE 5
20 GCOL 0,129      :REM (128+1)
30 CLG
   . . . .
```

You could now set a yellow foreground by a line such as:

        40 GCOL 0,2

2.5 Activities

---

i. See the effects of setting the foreground and background colours for graphics by entering the following in direct mode:

        MODE 5
        GCOL 0,129
        CLG
        GCOL 0,2
        DRAW 500,500
        GCOL 0,0
        DRAW 1280,500
        GCOL 0,3
        DRAW 500,1000

With a black and white television, you may need to adjust the contrast to distinguish the various shades of grey which correspond to the colours.

3 Drawing simple shapes

3.0 Introduction

The BBC Microcomputer provides a wide variety of plotting facilities. It can plot points, draw lines, and fill in areas - all in colour. With such a wide variety, it is not possible to have

0	move relative* to last point
1	draw line relative* in current graphics foreground colour
2	draw line relative* in the logical inverse colour
3	draw line relative* in current graphics background colour
4	move to absolute position
5	draw line absolute in current graphics foreground colour
6	draw line absolute in logical inverse colour
7	draw line absolute in current graphics background colour
+ 16	same effects as each of the above except that it plots a dotted line
+ 64	same effects as each of the above except that only a single point is plotted
+ 72	draw a horizontal line in both directions from the current point, reaching to the edges of the screen or to an area of non-background colour **
+ 80	same effects as each of the above except that it refers to filling in a triangular area between the specified point and the last two points used in plotting actions
+ 88	draw a horizontal line to the right of the current point, reaching to the right-hand edge of the screen or to an area of background colour **

* Plotting relative means that the computer considers the origin to be the previous point which it remembers. The true screen origin is still at (0,0).

** Only available on operating systems 1.0 onwards.

Table 3.1 Codes for N in the PLOT statement

individually named statements. Instead a single statement, controlled by a series of codes, provides for all of them. It is the PLOT statement. In this chapter, we explain the various ways in which you can use the PLOT statement.

3.1 Codes for the PLOT statement

The PLOT statement is very important in graphics. It has the following form, where N can have a wide range of values depending on the type of plot which is required; and X and Y refer to the co-ordinate to which you want to PLOT:

PLOT N,X,Y

For example the following version of the PLOT statement is equivalent to the DRAW statement:

PLOT 5,X,Y

Table 3.1 shows a simplified set of codes for N in the PLOT statement, together with the feature that it produces. To use Table 3.1, you must first decide what effects you want. You will probably want several simultaneously. You get them by adding up the codes for each one. For example, to draw a dotted line, select code 5 for a line and code 16 for a dotted effect. Since the total is 21, the code for a dotted line is 21.

Some of the more commonly used codes are as shown in Table 3.2. Most programs use only a small selection of these codes, such as 69 for plotting a point, 5 for drawing a line or 85

code	effect
4	equivalent of MOVE
5	equivalent of DRAW
21	draw dotted
69	plot a point
71	remove a point
85	fill a triangle
77	*'fill' a line

*For 1.0 operating systems onwards

Table 3.2 Most commonly used codes for N in the PLOT statement

for filling a triangular area. The last code (77) which applies only to models with the 1.0 or later operating systems, is said to 'fill' a line. This means that it draws a line in the current foreground colour, extending horizontally left and right until it reaches either the edge of the screen or a non-background colour. It is particularly suitable for filling in the colour of some irregularly shaped area. Nevertheless it is not a complete fill routine, as it only fills up irregularities on the left or right. It does not extend up and down. In the next activities there is an example of the 77 fill form of the PLOT statement.

You will find a program much easier to read if, at the beginning of the program, you define some aptly named variables such as:

	dot =69
or	line = 5
or	triangle =85

Then the PLOT statements further on in the program are much more readily recognizable because they appear as:

	PLOT dot,X,Y
or	PLOT line,X,Y
or	PLOT triangle,X,Y etc.

3.2 Activities

i. If you have a 1.0 or above operating system, you can get the feel of the fill form of the PLOT statement by running the following program. It uses the RND function in line 60 to mark out a random edge which is the left-hand edge of the block to be filled. PLOT77 is called by line 110 inside a FOR ... NEXT loop. (You can find out which version of the operating system you have by entering *FX0 which causes the number of your operating system to appear on the screen.)

```
10 MODE 5 :GCOL 0,129 :GCOL 0,2
20 CLG
30 REM Draw a random left-hand edge
40 MOVE 500,100
50 FOR Y=100 TO 1000 STEP 20
60    DRAW 200+RND(600),Y
70    NEXT Y
```

```
 80 MOVE 800,100
 90 REM Now for the fill routine
100 FOR Y=100 TO 1000 STEP 4
110    PLOT77,900,Y
120    NEXT Y
```

ii. Speed is an advantage when programming graphics. You can measure the speed of execution of a program by means of the BBC Microcomputer's TIME facility. Investigate the time of execution of the above program by running it with the following additional two lines:

```
  5 TIME = 0
130 PRINT TIME
```

We discuss this further in Section 3.5.

iii. One way of speeding up BASIC is to use integer variables in place of ordinary variables. For example, the above program can be speeded up by putting the integer variable Y% in place of Y. Use the editing facilities to change all occurrences of Y to Y% and re-run the program.

iv. We now show the use of an area-fill routine. The following program draws a series of circles and then fills in the area around them. The filling routine is written in BASIC but uses integer variables wherever possible to gain speed. In lines 290 and 310 there are references to GOTO, a statement which we have tried to avoid. Unfortunately the standard way round this, which is to use REPEAT ... UNTIL loops, is not possible because the recursive nature of the routine causes too many such loops. Enter the program and run it. You may like to record both the circle-drawing and the fill routines for your own use elsewhere.

```
 10 MODE4
 20 VDU19,0,4;0;
 30 VDU19,1,3;0;
 40 PROCcircle(640,512,500)
 50 PROCcircle(400,700,100)
 60 PROCcircle(900,700,100)
 70 PROCcircle(640,400,200)
 80 PROCfill(500,100)
 90 END
100 :
110 DEF PROCcircle(x,y,r)
```

```
120  st=2*PI/100
130  S=SIN(st) :C=COS(st)
140  xp=r :yp=0
150  MOVE  x+r,y
160  FOR L%=1 TO 200
170    xr=xp*C-yp*S
180    yp=xp*S+yp*C :xp=xr
190    DRAWx+xp,y+yp
200    NEXT L%
210  ENDPROC
220  :
230  DEF PROCfill(B%,C%)
240  LOCAL A%,X%,Y%,F%,O%
250  F%=&FFFF:A%=13:X%=&80:Y%=0:O%=&FFF1
260  PROCF:ENDPROC
270  DEF PROCF:PLOT&4D,B%,C%:CALLO%:
     LOCAL U%,V%:U%=!X%ANDF%
280  B%=U%:C%=C%+4:V%=X%!4 ANDF%
290  PLOT&5C,B%,C%:CALL O%:B%=X%!4+4ANDF%:
     IF V%>=B% THEN PROCF:GOTO290
300  B%=U%:C%=C%-8
310  PLOT&5C,B%,C%:CALL O%:B%=X%!4+4ANDF%:
     IF V%>=B% THEN PROCF:GOTO310
320  C%=C%+4:B%=V%:ENDPROC
```

3.3 Using the PLOT statement

As an example of the various applications of PLOT statements, you may like to examine the development of a program to draw a picture of a sailing boat. The display is very simply produced and is shown in Screen Display 3.1. The actual screen version looks much more interesting because it is in colour.

We assume that the boat is to be drawn anywhere on the screen using a procedure called PROCboat, which we define in terms of other procedures, as follows:

```
 60  DEFPROCboat(X,Y,s)
 70  GCOL0,1:PROCsails(X,Y)
 80  GCOL0,2:PROCmast(X,Y)
 90  GCOL0,3:PROCbase(X,Y)
100  ENDPROC
```

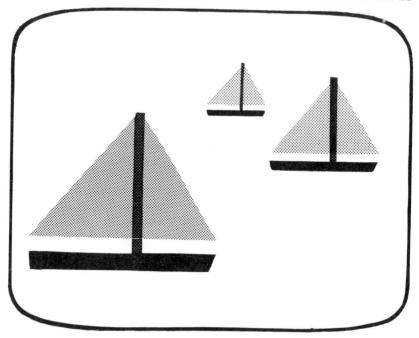

Screen Display 3.1

The numbers in the GCOL statements set the foreground colour to be red for the sails, green for the mast and yellow for the base.

We shall develop the procedure PROCsails first as it is the simplest. The sails are to be triangular in shape and so rely on PLOT triangle,X,Y. The same reference point X,Y will be chosen when calling each of the procedures, the size of the boat will be controlled by s. This means that we have to decide on the height of the sails above the reference point in terms of s. We call this 'sh' for sail height. The first sail is now drawn by two references to MOVE and one to PLOT triangle,X,Y. The references to MOVE are necessary as the graphics routine remembers the last two plotted points and draws the triangle between these and the current point. The PROCsails procedure becomes:

```
120 DEFPROCsails(x,y)
130 sb=10*s:fr=30*s:ba=40*s:sh=50*s
140 MOVE x+fr,y+sb
```

```
   Listing 3.1
10 MODE2:GCOL Ø,132 :CLG :REM
   For Model A use  mode 5
20 triangle=85
25 PROCboat(350,150,8)
30 PROCboat(700,700,4)
35 PROCboat(950,400,6)
40 END
50 :
60 DEFPROCboat(x,y,s)
70 GCOLØ,1:PROCsails(x,y)
80 GCOLØ,2:PROCmast(x,y)
90 GCOLØ,3:PROCbase(x,y)
100 ENDPROC
110 :
120 DEFPROCsails(x,y)
130 sb=1Ø*s:fr=3Ø*s:ba=4Ø*s:sh=5Ø*s
140 MOVE x+fr,y+sb
150 MOVE x-ba,y+sb
160 PLOT triangle,x,y+sh
170 ENDPROC
180 :
190 DEFPROCmast(x,y)
200 mw=s:mh=5Ø*s
210 MOVE x-mw,y:MOVE x+mw,y
220 PLOT triangle,x-mw,y+mh
230 PLOT triangle,x+mw,y+mh
240 ENDPROC
250 :
260 DEFPROCbase(x,y)
270 depth=7*s:fr=3Ø*s:ba=4Ø*s:lf=25*s
280 MOVE x+fr,y
290 MOVE x-ba,y
300 PLOT triangle,x+lf,y-depth
310 PLOT triangle,x-ba,y-depth
320 ENDPROC
```

```
150 MOVE x-ba,y+sb
160 PLOT triangle,x,y+sh
170 ENDPROC
```

In PROCsails the two sails are drawn as a single triangle, because the overlapping mast will separate them into two. PROCmast draws the mast as a narrow rectangular column by two calls to PLOTtriangle, as shown in lines 220 and 230. The width and height of the mast is set by 'mw' and 'mh' respectively in the following lines:

```
190 DEFPROCmast(x,y)
200 mw=s:mh=50*s
210 MOVE x-mw,y:MOVE x+mw,y
220 PLOT triangle,x-mw,y+mh
230 PLOT triangle,x+mw,y+mh
240 ENDPROC
```

The procedure for the base of the boat is given below and uses ideas similar to those for drawing triangular areas. The thickness of the base is set by the variable 'depth' and 'fr' and 'ba' are the distances to the front and the back. To give the angled prow, 'lf' is the distance to the lowest part of the boat at the front.

```
260 DEFPROCbase(x,y)
270 depth=7*s:fr=30*s:ba=40*s:lf=25*s
280 MOVE x+fr,y
290 MOVE x-ba,y
300 PLOT triangle,x+lf,y-depth
310 PLOT triangle,x-ba,y-depth
320 ENDPROC
```

The complete program is given in Listing 3.1. It has three calls to PROCboat and accordingly causes three boats to be displayed.

3.4 Activities

i. Enter the program in Listing 3.1 and run it.

ii. Try modifying lines 25, 30 and 35 as shown below, in order to produce simple animation for one of the boats.

```
25 FOR X=0 TO 600 STEP 4
30 PROCboat (X,512,4)
35 NEXT X
```

iii. Although the display illustrates nice animation for the front of the boat, a coloured smear is left behind it. See if you can find a way of removing it by developing a procedure called PROCrubout. We suggest a possibility in Section 3.5.

iv. Try writing a program to make the boat of Screen Display 3.1 move slowly across a green sea with its surface rippled like a sine wave. Can you program this? We give a possible program in Section 3.5.

3.5 Discussion of activities

Activity 3.2 ii: Inside the BBC Microcomputer is an accurate clock. It increments the variable TIME continously once the computer has been turned on. However, the value held in TIME can be reset by a program at any stage. The value of TIME is measured in hundredths of a second (centiseconds) from the start of the program where TIME is set to zero.

Activity 3.4 iii: The following is one possibility for PROCrubout:

```
340 DEF PROCrubout(x,y)
350 MOVE x-mw,y :DRAW x-mw,y+mh
360 DRAW x-ba,y+sb
370 DRAW x-ba,y-depth
380 ENDPROC
```

Its call would have to be preceded by a GCOL 0,4 statement, as follows, to set the colour to blue for redrawing the sky:

```
32 GCOL 0,4:PROCrubout(X,512)
```

Activity 3.4 iv: Below is one possible program to give a display of the boat sailing across a green sea, its surface rippled like a sine wave, against a blue sky.

```
10 MODE5:GCOL 0,123:CLG
20 triangle=85
22 PROCsea
```

```
25 FOR X=-120 TO 1500 STEP 8
30    PROCboat(X,512,4)
32    GCOL0,4:PROCrubout(X,512)
35    NEXT X
40 END
50 :
60 DEFPROCboat(x,y,s)
70 GCOL0,1:PROCsails(x,y)
80 GCOL0,2:PROCmast(x,y)
90 GCOL0,3:PROCbase(x,y)
100 ENDPROC
110 :
120 DEFPROCsails(x,y)
130 sb=10*s:fr=30*s:ba=40*s:sh=50*s
140 MOVE x+fr,y+sb
150 MOVE x-ba,y+sb
160 PLOT triangle,x,y+sh
170 ENDPROC
180 :
190 DEFPROCmast(x,y)
200 mw=s:mh=50*s
210 MOVE x-mw,y:MOVE x+mw,y
220 PLOT triangle,x-mw,y+mh
230 PLOT triangle,x+mw,y+mh
240 ENDPROC
250 :
260 DEFPROCbase(x,y)
270 depth=7*s:fr=30*s:ba=40*s:lf=25*s
280 MOVE x+fr,y
290 MOVE x-ba,y
300 PLOT triangle,x+lf,y-depth
310 PLOT triangle,x-ba,y-depth
320 ENDPROC
330 :
340 DEF PROCrubout(x,y)
350 MOVE x-mw,y :DRAW x-mw,y+mh
360 DRAW x-ba,y+sb
370 DRAW x-ba,y-depth
380 ENDPROC
390 :
400 DEF PROCsea
410 GCOL0,2
420 FOR X=0 TO 1280 STEP 8
430    MOVE X,0 :DRAW X,450+50*SIN(X/40)
```

```
440   NEXT X
450 ENDPROC
```

4 Programming your own characters

4.0 Introduction

In the normal way, the BBC Microcomputer can only print those characters whose shapes are stored in memory. These are the set of numbers 0-9, the set of lower case letters a-z, the set of upper case letters A-Z, and a few others such as punctuation

42

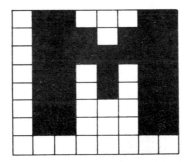

Figure 4.1a. The character M, showing the matrix into which it fits (not to scale).

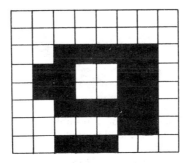

Figure 4.1b. The character g, showing the matrix into which it fits (not to scale).

marks. The BBC Microcomputer does not provide characters for shapes, such as hearts, pin-men and space invaders, but it does allow you to program your own. Such characters are available in all display modes other than mode 7 and are called programmable characters. Furthermore by joining up programmable characters, you can produce larger, composite figures. Consequently you can design figures to the shape and size of your choosing! This is an exciting and powerful facility, which you will probably want to use a lot for graphics programming. Its application is limited only by your imagination. This chapter describes how to do it.

4.1 Designing a programmable character

Every character has to be made from spots (pixels) arranged within a matrix of eight rows and eight columns. Figures 4.1a and b show these pixels in highly magnified pictures of the characters M and g (not to scale). You will see that they do not extend through the full height and width of the matrix. There are two reasons for this. Firstly there has to be at least one column spare to prevent characters touching when several are written together; and secondly, some lower case characters, like g and y, need tails. These are called 'descenders' and they alone can occupy the bottom row.

When you come to design a programmable character, you should bear in mind that it has to fit within the eight by eight matrix. You may wish to use all the matrix. Then your programmed character will be very slightly bigger than a keyboard character.

Figure 4.2a. The first stage in designing a programmed character: designing the character.

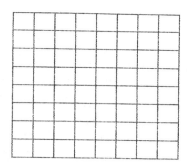

Figure 4.2b. The second stage in designing a programmed character: drawing an eight by eight matrix.

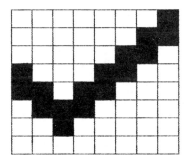

Figure 4.2c. The third stage in designing a programmed character: integrating the character in the matrix.

However, it will not look significantly bigger on the screen. So any fine detail will be too small to show - and it is worth remembering this! (We show you how to make a larger, more complex figure in Section 4.6).

The first step in designing a programmable character is to decide on its shape. We can illustrate the process with a simple tick, as shown in Figure 4.2a. The next step is to draw out a grid of rectangles with eight rows and eight columns, as shown in Figure 4.2b. The final step is to draw the shape - in this case, the tick - onto the grid as a set of blobs, as shown in Figure 4.2c. At this stage the smooth lines of the original figure have to be translated into the step-like edges of the pixels. This is a matter of trial, error and compromise.

4.2 Converting the design to code

In order to feed the character into the computer, you have to reduce its shape to numbers. One method involves translating the blobs of each row of the figure into the 1's and 0's of a binary number, taking a background blob as 0 and a foreground blob as 1 - and in the next paragraph we describe the process. However, if you find it tedious, you may prefer to skip to the paragraph after, because it describes a 'formula' by which you can much more simply achieve the same result. Alternatively, in Activities 4.3, we supply a program which does the whole thing for you.

The computer stores each line of a character as an eight bit binary number (a total of eight 0's and 1's). The binary number representing the top row of the tick is 00000001, which is 1 in numbers to the base ten. A single 1 in the second position gives

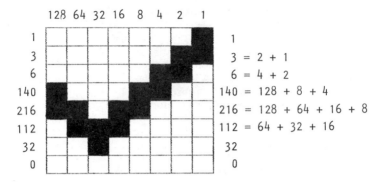

Figure 4.2d. Turning the programmed character into codes.

the binary number 00000010, which is 2 in base ten numbers. If both squares are occupied, the binary representation is 00000011, which is 3 i.e. the sum of the previous two.

Now for the 'formula'. You can take each column of the matrix as having a value: 1 for the right-most column, 2 for the next column, 4 for the next, 8 for the next, etc. These values are shown along the top of the matrix in Figure 4.2d. To reduce the character to code, all you have to do is to add up the values for each row of the figure for the positions which should be lit up. By way of example, the numbers on the right of Figure 4.2d show these sums for each row of the tick. These are the codes which have to be fed into the computer.

All that remains is to instruct the computer to accept the codes to represent a character. This is the function of the VDU23 statement. It instructs the computer to accept the coded numbers into its memory as the newly designed character. You use the statement in the following way, where 'row1' represents the code for row 1, etc., and 'character' is the ASCII code for the character:

> VDU 23,character,row1,row2,row3,row4,row5,row6,
> row7,row8

Thus to reprogram ASCII character 224 as the tick would require the following statement, where the string of eight numbers after the VDU 23,224 represents the numbers for the rows as shown in Figure 4.2d:

> VDU 23,224,1,3,6,140,216,112,32,0

A word about the ASCII codes: in normal operation ASCII codes 0 - 31 inclusive are reserved for controlling the video display. Therefore you cannot normally use any of these for programming characters. ASCII codes 32 - 127 are for the normal keyboard display; so you would not normally want to redefine them. Appendix 3 gives the ASCII codes. ASCII codes 224 - 255 inclusive are the most suitable for reprogramming.

You can normally only use a block of 32 at any one time. These blocks are: codes 32 - 63, 64 - 95, 96 - 127, 128 - 159, 160 - 191 and 192 - 223. With the exception of the keyboard characters, one block duplicates any other. For example, if you print CHR$(224), you get the same character as if you had printed CHR$(128), CHR$(160) and CHR$(192).

4.3 Activities

Listing 4.1 gives a program which allows you to design and edit your own programmable character. You merely have to use the cursor-control keys to move the cursor to that part of the grid that you want to fill, and then press 1. You can edit the character by pressing 0 to change your mind. Screen Display 4.1 shows a stage during the editing of a character.

4.4 Printing programmable characters

Programmable characters can only be printed on the screen in modes 0 to 6. Mode 7 has its own character set which cannot be altered.

You will be familiar with the simplest way of printing a character. Taking the character M as an example, this is:

PRINT "M"

An alternative way is to use the statement CHR$, together with the ASCII code for that character. Again taking M as an example, this would be as follows:

PRINT CHR$(77)

The shape for each character you redefine is stored in the computer's memory until the computer is either switched off, or the character is defined as something else. The definition of each of the standard characters is stored in ROM, but any characters that you reprogram must be stored in the volatile memory that holds BASIC programs. By special instructions the computer can be forced to hold a reprogrammed version of most of its characters, but this takes up even more memory space and we will not go into it here.

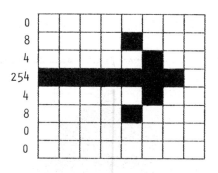

VDU 23,224,0,8,4,254,4,8,0,0

Figure 4.3a. A programmed figure with its VDU definition.

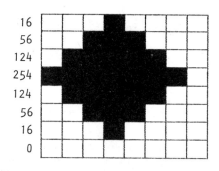

VDU 23,224,16,56,124,254,124,56,16,0

Figure 4.3b. A programmed figure with its VDU definition.

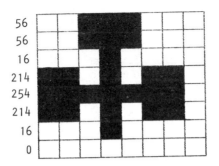

VDU 23,224,56,56,16,214,254,214,16,0

Figure 4.3c. A programmed figure with its VDU definition.

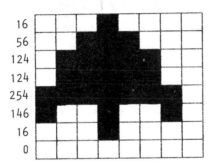

VDU 23,224,16,56,124,124,254,146,16,0

Figure 4.3d. A programmed figure with its VDU definition.

4.5 Activities

i. We suggest that you now try making some programmed characters. You can do it in any mode except mode 7. As it takes some time to think out characters and redefine them, we help by supplying a small library of shapes for you. These are shown in Figure 4.3a,b,c,d,e,f,g, together with the corresponding VDU definitions. Our library uses the same character code, 224,

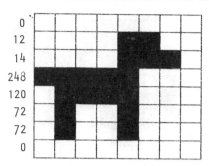

VDU 23,224,0,12,14,248,120,72,72,0

Figure 4.3e. A programmed figure with its VDU definition.

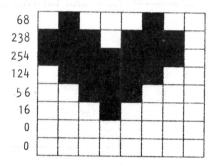

VDU 23,224,68,238,254,124,56,16,0,0

Figure 4.3f. A programmed figure with its VDU definition.

for each character, but you should use a variety unless you are prepared for one character to overwrite another. Any number between 224 and 255 is suitable.

Use the VDU 23 statement to define a character code as each of the characters in our library. Then print it using a statement such as:

PRINT CHR$(224)

ii. You may like to try programming some characters of your own.

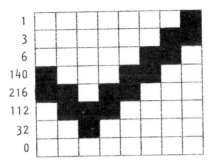

VDU 23,224,1,3,6,140,216,112,32,0

Figure 4.3g. A programmed figure with its VDU definition.

4.6 Composite figures

Frequently the size of a single character is just too small to give a realistic image on the screen. Then you need to make a larger figure, consisting of a number of programmed characters together. This section introduces a routine to print such composite figures.

Each character making up the composite figures has to be programmed as described above. These characters can then be printed together on any one line by including them in the same PRINT statement, separated by semicolons. Thus, printing the three characters 224, 225 and 226 side by side would require the statement:

PRINT CHR$(224);CHR$(225);CHR$(226)

This can be written more compactly using the VDU statement:

VDU 224,225,226

This can be written even more compactly by making the characters 224, 225, 226 into a string, as follows:

composite$ = CHR$(224)+CHR$(225)+CHR$(226)

You can now produce the composite figure with:

PRINT composite$

To write one set of characters directly under another set requires use of the cursor control codes. The ASCII codes for moving the cursor are shown in Table 4.1:

ASCII code	result
08	move backwards one space
09	move forward one space
10	move down one line
11	move up one line

Table 4.1 Cursor control codes

```
VDU 23,224,15,16,32,64,94,162,156,129
VDU 23,225,240,8,4,2,122,69,57,129
VDU 23,226,129,129,131,88,79,39,16,15
VDU 23,227,129,129,193,26,242,228,8,240
```

Figure 4.4a. A composite figure with its VDU definitions.

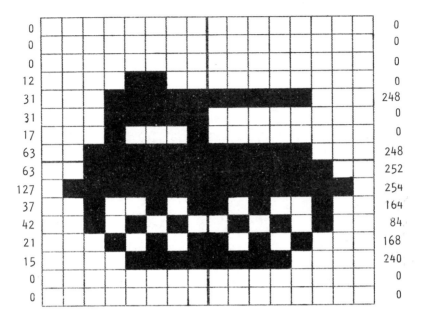

```
VDU  23,224,0,0,0,12,31,31,17,63
VDU  23,225,0,0,0,0,248,0,0,248
VDU  23,226,63,127,37,42,21,15,0,0
VDU  23,227,252,254,164,84,168,240,0,0
```

Figure 4.4b. A composite figure with its VDU definitions.

A second row of three characters could be printed directly underneath, if the cursor is first moved down one line followed by three spaces to the left. This can be achieved with the code 10 (for cursor down one line) followed by three lots of the code 8 (for cursor to move backwards one space, three times). Once again you can combine all these charactes, together with the control codes, into a single string, as follows:

```
composite$ =  CHRS$(224)+CHRS$(225)+CHRS$(226)+
              CHRS$(10)+CHRS$(8)+CHRS$(8)+
              CHRS$(8)+CHRS$(227)+CHRS$(228)+
              CHRS$(229)
```

4.7 Activities

i. You may like to try programming some composite figures of your own. However, because it takes some time to think them out and program them, we have helped by supplying a small

```
 10 REM The professor
 20 VDU23,224,0,0,1,1,2,1,2,6
 30 VDU23,225,66,129,0,152,185,203,87,163
 40 VDU23,226,0,0,128,128,128,128,128,0
 50 VDU23,227,2,3,7,15,5,1,3,6
 60 VDU23,228,131,6,68,154,225,136,32,0
 70 VDU23,229,0,0,0,0,0,0,128,0
 80 VDU23,230,14,12,16,0,32,0,64,64
 90 VDU23,231,0,0,0,4,0,2,1,6
100 VDU23,232,64,32,16,8,4,132,8,16
110 VDU23,233,128,128,128,128,128,128,128,128
120 VDU23,234,8,24,14,19,18,12,0,0
130 VDU23,235,32,64,128,32,32,16,8,48
140 VDU23,236,128,123,4,10,17,32,64,128
150 VDU23,237,0,251,1,1,0,128,64,96
160 VDU23,238,192,0,0,0,128,64,32,16
170 VDU23,239,57,78,79,63,31,15,7,3
180 VDU23,240,0,1,2,132,200,240,240,224
190 VDU23,241,144,8,4,3,3,4,12,15
200 VDU23,242,24,60,254,254,252,248,240,224
210
220 MODE 5
230 COLOUR 129:COLOUR 2
240 CLS
250 PRINTTAB(17,12):PROCPROF
260 PRINTTAB(0,31);:END
270 DEF PROCPROF
280 VDU 32,224,225,226
290 VDU 10,08,08,08,227,228,229
300 VDU 10,08,08,08,230,231,232
310 VDU 10,08,08,08,233,234,235
320 VDU 10,08,08,08,236,237,238
330 VDU 10,08,08,08,08,239,240,241,242
340 ENDPROC
```

Figure 4.4c. A composite figure with its VDU definitions and a program for drawing it.

library for you to use. These are shown in Figure 4.4a, b and c, together with the corresponding VDU definitions and the procedures for the drawing.

ii. Although the result may seem a little jerky, try moving these composites around the screen using the TAB statement to locate them. We give a possible program in Section 4.10.

4.8 Multicoloured characters and figures

You can make your programmable characters and figures multicoloured. The technique relies on VDU5. Although the main function of VDU5 is to allow the character to be printed at the graphics cursor, it also has the subtle effect of only writing foreground. This means that several characters can be printed at the same place without each destroying the other. VDU5 is turned off by VDU4 which returns writing to the text cursor.

Suppose you want a character to be red, green and blue. You merely define three separate characters: the first representing the red, the second the green and the third the blue. Then you write the first with the foreground set to red; the second with the foreground set to green and the third with the foreground set to blue.

For example, you can get a two-coloured T with the following lines of program:

```
10 MODE5
20 VDU5
30 VDU23,224,255,255,0,0,0,0,0,0
40 VDU23,225,0,0,24,24,24,24,24,24
50 GCOL 0,1 :MOVE 500,500
60 PRINT CHR$(224)
70 GCOL 0,2 :MOVE 500,500
80 PRINT CHR$(225)
90 VDU4
100 END
```

PROGRAM TO DEFINE A CHARACTER

Use the cursor-control keys to position
the cursor. Then press 1 if you want to
fill the square. Press Ø to change back.

Character definition =
VDU 23,224,252,192,168,144,136,132,2,1

Appearance of character = ▚

Screen Display 4.1 (If your computer has a 0.1 operating system, the cursor keys cannot be used as instructed in the Screen Display. Use the following alternative keys: H to move left; J to move right; Q to move down; and A to move up.)

4.9 Activities

i. Use the technique described in the previous section to make some of your own multicoloured characters and composite figures.

ii. What is the maximum number of colours that can theoretically fit into any one character? (See Section 4.10.)

```
   Listing 4.1
10 MODE 4 :VDU19,0,4;0; :VDU19,1,3;0;
20 REM Clear character matrix
30 DIM CHAR(8,8)
40 PRINT ' "        PROGRAM TO DEFINE A CHARACTER"
50 PRINT ' "Use the cursor-control keys to position"
60 PRINT"the cursor. Then press 1 if you want to"
70 PRINT"fill the square. Press 0 to change back."
80 BASEX=340 :YBASE=790 :S=72
90 N=0 :X=0 :Y=0 :tr=85 :D=8
100 PROCDISPLAY
110 *FX4,2
120 *KEY12 H
130 *KEY13 J
140 *KEY14 Q
150 *KEY15 A
160 REPEAT
170   REPEAT
180     K=ASC(INKEY$(5))-73 :IF K=-74 THEN PROCdisplay
190     IF K=-24 OR K=-25 THEN CHAR(X,Y)=K+25 :K=0
200   UNTIL (ABS(K)=1 OR ABS(K)=8 OR K=0) AND N+K>=0
          AND N+K<64
210   N=N+K
220   PROCsetchar
230   PROCdisplay
240 UNTIL 1=2
250 :
260 DEF PROCsetchar
270 X=N MOD 8 :Y=N DIV 8
280 CHAR(8,Y)=0
290 FOR I=0 TO 7
300   IF CHAR(I,Y)=1 THEN CHAR(8,Y)=CHAR(8,Y)+2^(7-I)
310   NEXT I
320 PRINT TAB(0,26);"Character definition =" ' ' "VDU
      23,224";
330 FORI=0 TO 7 :PRINT ",";CHAR(8,I); :NEXT
340   VDU23,224
350   FOR J=0 TO 7 :PRINT CHR$(CHAR(8,J)); :NEXT J
      :PRINT"       "                          P.T.O.
360   ENDPROC
```

Listing 4.1 continued

```
370    :
380    DEF PROCdisplay
390    PRINT TAB(0,30);"Appearance of character = ";
       CHR$(224)
400    IF CHAR(X,Y)=1 THEN PROCNGT :PROCONE ELSE
       PROCONE :PROCNGT
410    ENDPROC
420    END
430    :
440    DEF PROCDISPLAY
450    FOR N=63 TO 0 STEP -1
460      X=N MOD 8 :Y=N DIV 8
470      IF CHAR(X,Y)=1 THEN PROCONE ELSE PROCONE
         :PROCNGT
480      NEXT N
490    ENDPROC
500    :
510    DEF PROCONE
520    GCOL0,131
530    VDU24,BASEX+X*S;YBASE-S-Y*S;BASEX+S+X*S;
       YBASE-Y*S;
540    CLG
550    ENDPROC
560    :
570    DEF PROCNGT
580    GCOL0,128
590    VDU24,BASEX+D+X*S;YBASE+D-S-Y*S;BASEX-D+S+X*S;
       YBASE-D-Y*S;
600    CLG
610    ENDPROC
```

4.10 Discussion of activities

Activities 4.7ii:

```
10 MODE5
20 VDU23,224,0,0,0,12,31,31,17,63
30 VDU23,225,0,0,0,0,248,0,0,248
40 VDU23,226,63,127,37,42,21,15,0,0
```

```
 50 VDU23,227,252,254,164,84,168,240,0,0
 60 tank$=CHR$(32)+CHR$(224)+CHR$(225)+CHR$(10)+
    CHR$(8)+CHR$(8)+CHR$(8)+CHR$(32)+CHR$(226)+
    CHR$(227)
 70 FOR X=0 TO 19
 80    PRINT TAB(X,20);tank$
 90    T=TIME :REPEAT UNTIL TIME=T+50
100    NEXT X
110 END
```

The ASCII code 32 in line 60 prints a space. This is necessary to rub out the back of the tank.

Activities 4.9ii: The number depends on the mode. For example, in a four-colour mode you can have three foreground colours. So you can have three colours in any one character.

5 Animating displays

5.0 Introduction

You can animate a graphics display, by making a series of pictures appear and disappear in quick succession. The effectiveness depends on how quickly you can make each picture change. The quickest way is to redefine the colours, so that

0 = black	8 = flashing black/white
1 = red	9 = flashing red/cyan
2 = green	10 = flashing green/magenta
3 = yellow	11 = flashing yellow/blue
4 = blue	12 = flashing blue/yellow
5 = magenta	13 = flashing magenta/green
6 = cyan	14 = flashing cyan/red
7 = white	15 = flashing white/black

Table 5.1 The colours of the absolute colour numbers

whole areas of one colour turn into other colours virtually instantaneously. This chapter describes how to redefine colours and how to use the technique to produce animation.

5.1 The redefinable and absolute colour numbers: a summary

You have already used the COLOUR statement to specify the foreground and background colours for text and the GCOL statement for graphics. You will recall that each requires a colour number which we called a redefinable colour number (see Section 2.1). We shall now summarise the essential differences between redefinable colour numbers and absolute colour numbers.

An absolute colour number is the number of the colour which is to be reproduced on the screen. It is like a name, by which any colour can be unambiguously referred and it can never be changed, irrespective of the screen mode in operation. Table 5.1 lists the absolute colour numbers.

A redefinable colour number is the colour number which appears in the COLOUR and GCOL statements. Its effect depends on the screen mode in operation at the time and on whether or not it has been redefined. When a redefinable colour has not been redefined, the following operate by default:

For modes 0 and 4:

        redefinable colour 0 = absolute colour 0 (black)
        redefinable colour 1 = absolute colour 7 (white)

For modes 1 and 5:

        redefinable colour 0 = absolute colour 0 (black)
        redefinable colour 1 = absolute colour 1 (red)
        redefinable colour 2 = absolute colour 3 (yellow)
        redefinable colour 3 = absolute colour 7 (white)

For mode 2 the redefinable colour number has a default value equal to the absolute colour number given in Table 5.1.

5.2 Redefining colours

The command to change the definition of a colour number is VDU19. Its form is as follows, where the semicolons control how BASIC interprets numbers and should not be confused with commas:

        VDU19,redefinable colour,absolute colour;0;

For example, the following would redefine the redefinable colour number 0 to be the absolute colour number 4, to give blue:

        VDU19,0,4;0;

As soon as you enter this line, every point on the screen which was originally written in the redefinable colour 0 becomes blue. As 0 corresponds to the background which, by default is black for all modes, this provides a blue background for all writing on the screen.
    The writing on the screen in a four-colour mode can be made yellow by the following:

        VDU19,3,3;0;

The redefinable colour numbers are automatically reset to the default when the mode is changed, or by the statement VDU 20, or by control/T.

5.3 Activities

For a quick and easy way to see the effects of redefining colour numbers, define the first red user-definable key to set the redefinable colour 0 to 7; define the second user-definable key to set the redefinable colour 1 to 0; and set the third user-definable key to reset the redefinable colours i.e. 0 (background) to 0 (black) and 1 (foreground) to 7 (white). To do this, you need the following lines, entered in direct mode:

```
*KEY0 VDU19,0,7;0;¦M
*KEY1 VDU19,1,0;0;¦M
*KEY2 VDU20¦M
```

Also change the mode to mode 4 by entering MODE4. This resets the redefinable colours and switches to a two-colour mode with redefinable colour 0=black and 1=white.

i. Now enter any message on the screen, just to get some writing there. (Ignore the error message.) Is the writing in its normal form of white writing on a black background?

ii. Next press the user-definable key f0. As the key redefines the redefinable colour 0 to be white, does the screen turn uniformly white?

iii. Next press the user-definable key f1. As the key redefines the redefinable colour 1 as black, does it cause the writing on the screen to reappear, this time as black writing on a white background?

iv. Finally press the user-definable key f2. Does it bring the system back to normal?

v. What would have happened if you had done this activity in a four colour mode? We discuss this in Section 5.9.

5.4 Animation

To produce an animated picture requires you to display, in rapid succession, independent and slightly different views, each showing a progression from the previous one. When they are presented quickly, one after the other, the result can give the illusion of movement. Although it is impossible, with present technology, for home computers to produce the equivalent of a cinema film, attractive results can be obtained. The computer has to work out a number of images and store them in memory. Then it has to arrange to switch from one to another in rapid succession to give the impression of movement. The process of redefining colours enables this succession to be sufficiently rapid, and we describe it here.

It is best to start by defining all the redefinable colours on the screen to be background, and so by default black. Then you draw a suitable number of successive images, by drawing each in a separate colour number. The number of redefinable colour numbers, and therefore the number of images, depends on the display mode, i.e. 0 to 3 for modes 1 and 5, 0 to 15 for mode 2. Each image can now be viewed, if you define its particular redefinable colour number as white, keeping all others black. Then you can switch between one view and another by selecting which redefinable colour to define as white while keeping all others as black.

Essentially each available redefinable colour number can be used to draw a different frame of the final animated picture. To hide any one frame, its redefinable colour is defined as the background colour. Thus one colour number (usually 0) has to be reserved for the background colour and is therefore unavailable for drawing a frame. So, in a four colour mode, it is possible to draw three individual frames, each of which can be turned on or off. In the eight + eight colour mode, it is possible to draw fifteen independent frames. Clearly this produces the best animation, but you need a Model B.

This type of animation cannot be done in the two-colour graphics modes, 0 and 4. With only two colours, either nothing or all parts of the picture are visible.

5.5 Activities

---

i. To see the effects of animation by colour redefinition, enter Listing 5.1, which produces an animated picture of a tap dripping into a tray which slowly fills up. Screen Display 5.1 cannot do justice to the animation on the actual screen, which shows the drips falling from the tap. Each *FX19 in lines 240 - 260 of the listing force the program to wait until the start of the next display frame on the television. We use it here as a method of producing a time delay and for getting better animation. This program only works on a Model B.

ii. Try to adapt the program by speeding up the drips or by altering the rate at which the tray fills up.

5.6 Overlapping images

For the animation which we have just described, each image must be separate from the others. If any parts of the images overlap then the one which is placed on the screen last overwrites the previous one. If this is unacceptable, there is an alternative way of treating the image which allow as much overlap as necessary. This method allows only two separate images in mode 1 and 5 and four separate images in mode 2. We now describe it.

Within the computer all numbers are expressed by electrical signals which are either on or off, and the redefinable colour numbers are also expressed this way. For ease of expression, computer experts speak of signals as being either 1 or 0 to represent the on and off states. You can therefore specify any number in terms of the 1's and 0's that specify the signals inside the computer. We shall describe the process, as it works within mode 2. Consequently sixteen different colour numbers can be used. The computer specifies a colour number between 0 and 15 in terms of 1's and 0's, according to Table 5.2.

colour number	binary number
0	0000
1	0001
2	0010
3	0011
4	0100
5	0101
6	0110
7	0111
8	1000
9	1001
10	1010
11	1011
12	1100
13	1101
14	1110
15	1111

Table 5.2 Equivalent binary numbers and colour numbers

You will find that the following are the most important equivalents:

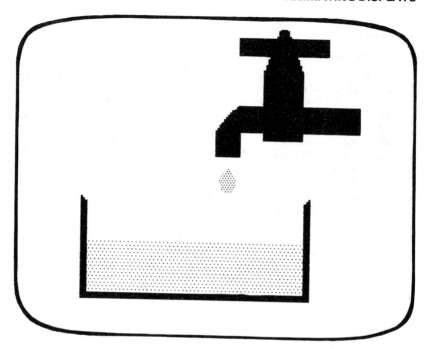

Screen Display 5.1

Normal colour 1 is equivalent to computer version 0001
Normal colour 2 is equivalent to computer version 0010
Normal colour 4 is equivalent to computer version 0100
Normal colour 8 is equivalent to computer version 1000

You will notice that each of these numbers uses a single 1 representing a single 'on' signal. Inside the computer there are four wires representing the colour in which you are drawing the picture. Also in the screen memory there are four separate cells in the screen memory chips which hold these four digits; they are either on or off. Each is independent of the others, which is important to remember when representing images. (Note that 1=0001 is independent of 2=0010 but that 3=0011, being a combination of 1 and 2, is dependent on both.) For overlapping pictures and for other pictorial effects, each of the four possible views of the picture need to be drawn, each in one of the four possible independent electrical positions, i.e. 0001, 0010, 0100 or 1000.

```
    Listing 5.1

 10 MODE2
 20 VDU19,8,2;0;
 30 FOR D=1 TO 5
 40    REM Draw drop
 50    GCOL0,D
 60    VDU19,D,0;0;
 70    VDU29,704;680-D*100;
 80    MOVE -30,0
 90    MOVE 0,50
100    PLOT 85,30,0
110    FOR A=0 TO 1.2 STEP.2
120       MOVE 0,0
130       PLOT 85,COS(A*PI)*30,
          -SIN(A*PI)*40
140       NEXT A
150    NEXT D
160 GCOL0,7
170 PROCtap(660,568,30)
180 PROCbeaker
190 F=80
200 REPEAT
210    REM Animate
220    FOR C=1 TO 5
230       VDU19,C,2;0;
240       *FX19
250       *FX19
260       *FX19
270       VDU19,C,0;0;
280       NEXT C
290    F=F+4
300    GCOL0,8
310    MOVE 168,F
320    DRAW 992,F
330    UNTIL F=400
340 :
350 END
360 :
```

```
       Listing 5.1 continued

370 DEF PROCtap(X,Y,S)
380 REM Move origin to X,Y
390 VDU29,X;Y;
400 MOVE S*18,S*3
410 MOVE S*18,S*6
420 PLOT 85,S*3,S*3
430 PLOT 85,S*3,S*6
440 PLOT 85,S*1.5,S*5
450 PLOT 85,S*3,0
460 PLOT 85,0,S*3
470 PLOT 85,0,0
480 MOVE S*6,S*2
490 MOVE S*11,S*2
500 PLOT 85,S*6,S*10
510 PLOT 85,S*11,S*10
520 PLOT 85,S*8.5,S*16
530 :
540 MOVE S*3,S*12
550 MOVE S*14,S*12
560 PLOT 85,S*3,S*14
570 PLOT 85,S*14,S*14
580 VDU29,0;0;
590 ENDPROC
600 :
610 DEFPROCbeaker
620 MOVE 160,400
630 MOVE 148,420
640 PLOT 85,160,80
650 PLOT 85,148,60
660 PLOT 85,1000,80
670 PLOT 85,1020,60
680 PLOT 85,1000,400
690 PLOT 85,1020,420
700 ENDPROC
```

Provided you draw the pictures in such a way that you do not rub out anything already on the screen, an overlap between a picture drawn in redefinable colour 1 (0001) with one drawn in redefinable colour 4 (0100), produces, at that position on the screen, the electrical code 0101 which is clearly a combination of the previous two.

You could have colour number 1 (0001) for an image of a man and 4 (0100) for the image of a tree. If you define 1 (0001) as red, then anywhere on the screen where you put the man, using the previous graphics techniques, the image will appear red. If, however, you can arrange that where the tree (0100) and the man (0001) overlap on the screen, the duality of the situation is recorded as tree (0100) + man (0001) = (0101), then you have the following possibilities: If this combined effect (0101) is defined as having the same colour as the tree (0100), then the man is not seen, i.e. he appears to have gone behind the tree! If the combined effect (0101) is defined as having the same colour as the man (0001) then this part of the tree will not be seen, i.e. he appears to have gone in front of the tree!

These manipulations require some knowledge of the the exclusive OR binary logic for combining numbers. We introduce it in the next section.

5.7 Logical operations

The logical operations are methods of performing what must appear at first sight to be nothing but rather strange arithmetic. Yet this type of arithmetic is crucial for computers. As we mentioned, all numbers inside the computer are dealt with as binary numbers and all binary numbers are a series of 1's and 0's. Essentially the binary operations are a way of combining the 1's and 0's of binary arithmetic. The operation which is required for animation uses the operator called 'the exclusive OR' which is written as XOR. The binary XOR operator combines 1's and 0's in the following way:

$$0 \text{ XOR } 0 = 0$$
$$1 \text{ XOR } 0 = 1$$
$$0 \text{ XOR } 1 = 1$$
$$1 \text{ XOR } 1 = 0$$

To illustrate the operation, consider two binary numbers, each represented by a combination of four 1's or 0's, such as the 0100 and 0001 of the previous section. To combine these two numbers using the logical XOR operator requires that one number be written above the other like this:

```
0100
0001
```

You now operate the logical XOR between the 1's and 0's in each column to give the result 0101. Thus, if you draw one picture on the screen using colour number 4 (0100) and then manage to draw another on the screen using colour 1 (0001) - this time making sure that the second picture does not overwrite the previous but is combined with it using the logical XOR function - then at every point on the screen where you have an overlap between 4 (0100) and 1 (0001) you get the number (0101) which is 5. You now have areas from the first picture which are in colour number 4 (0100), areas from the second picture in colour number 1 (0001) and areas where the two overlap, which are in colour number 5 (0101). You now only need to define colour number 5 to be the same as 4 or 1 and one image appears to be hidden by the other, where they overlap. The information that the two images do overlap is not lost, however, as the situation does have the different colour number 5 (0101) on the screen.

To remove one of the images from a particular area of the screen as would be required if a man was to be shown walking across the screen merely requires that his image be written to the same spot, a second time still using the logical XOR function.

This happens as 1 XOR 1 = 0. This means that 0101 XOR 0001 = 0100 which, in terms of the image, means that:

'overlapping image' XOR 'one of images'　　　= 'other image'

i.e.
```
0101          XOR          0001      =      0100
```

GCOL 3,C (where C is the colour number) is a statement which sets up the BBC Microcomputer to do the XOR operation. Once this statement has been executed, all future graphics displays will be of colours such that they are the XOR between the colour number that you are plotting and that already on the screen.

Screen Display 5.2

5.8 Activities

Screen Display 5.2 shows a tank and a pyramid. As it uses the complete range of colour numbers, it will only work on a Model B. Enter the program of Listing 5.2. Do you see the tank move behind the pyramid? Change the program and re-run it to show the tank moving in front of the pyramid.

```
   Listing 5.2
10 VDU23,255, 0,0,0,12,31,31,17,63
20 VDU23,254, 0,0,0,0,248,0,0,248
30 VDU23,253, 63,127,37,42,21,15,0,0
40 VDU23,252, 252,254,164,84,168,240,0,0
50 tank$=CHR$(255)+CHR$(254)+CHR$(10)+CHR$(8)+CHR$(8)
   +CHR$(253)+CHR$(252)
60 :
70 MODE2 :VDU19,0,4;0; :REM A blue sky
80 :
90 REM Now some green ground
100 GCOL0,2:MOVE 0,0:MOVE 1280,0
110 PLOT85,0,512:PLOT85,1280,512
120 :
130 REM a cyan pyramid
140 GCOL0,1 :VDU19,1,6;0;
150 MOVE 200,360:MOVE 600,360:PLOT85,400,660
160 :
170 REM A yellow pyramid
180 GCOL0,4 :VDU19,4,3;0;
190 MOVE 400,200 :MOVE 1000,200 :PLOT85,700,700
200 :
210 REM Now redefine tank colour combinations
220 VDU19,10,0;0;  :REM tank + ground = black
230 VDU19,9,0;0;   :REM tank + pyramid= black
240 VDU19,12,3;0;  :REM tank + pyramid= pyramid colour
250 :
260 REM Move tank
270 VDU5 :GCOL 3,8
280 *FX19
290 REPEAT
300    FOR I=1 TO 280 STEP 2
310       MOVE I*4,400 :PRINT tank$
320       FOR T=1 TO 100 :NEXT
330        MOVE I*4,400 :PRINT tank$
340       NEXT I
350    UNTIL 1=2
```

5. 9 Discussion of activities

Activity 5.3 v: If you had done the activity in a four colour mode, you could have redefined any of the four redefinable colour numbers 0, 1, 2 and 3 to be any of the absolute colours. This redefinition of redefinable colour numbers could have included redefining all of the colour numbers to represent black. Then the screen would become black whatever was drawn on it. Alternatively all of the redefinable colour numbers could have been defined as black, with the exception of one which could have been defined as white. Then only those parts of the picture which were drawn in the last redefinable colour would have been visible.

6 Drawing three dimensional ripple surfaces

6.0 Introduction

You have probably admired the three dimensional pictures that computers can draw. This chapter is about those beautifully symmetrical and shaded pictures of ripple surfaces, and it shows you how easy it is to design and draw them yourself.

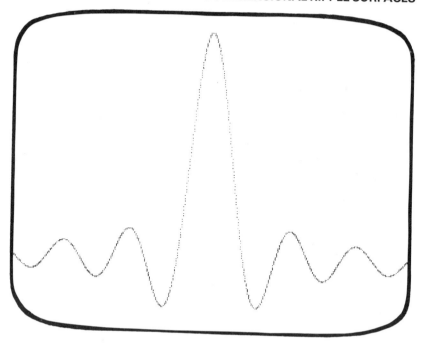

Screen Display 6.1

6.1 Choosing a function and scaling it

A three dimensional ripple surface can be built up from any suitable function. Any one will do as long as it can be written in terms recognisable to BASIC. So, to draw one for yourself, you must first choose a function. We explain the process using a function which, incidentally, derives from optics, where it represents the amplitude of light penetrating through a pin hole onto a screen behind:

SIN(R)/R

You can get an idea of the general shape of this function by plotting it in a suitable graphics mode, in two dimensions as a simple graph. This particular function has a maximum value of 1 where R=0 and a minimum value of about -0.2 so you have to scale up the values worked out for SIN(R)/R before you can plot

```
Listing 6.1
10 REM Display of SIN(X)/X
20 MODE4
25 VDU19,0,4;0;19,1,3;0;
30 point=69
40 VDU29,640;200; :REM Set origin
50 FOR X=-640.1 TO 640 STEP 2
60    PLOTpoint,X,800*32*SIN(X/32)/X
70    NEXT X
80 END
```

with a suitable size to fill the screen. If you scale the whole function up, by multiplying by 800, it will fit on the screen nicely. Listing 6.1 gives a program to display the two dimensional shape of this function. Screen Display 6.1 is the result.

As you see, the program uses the point-plotting version of the PLOT statement. Line 40 uses the following special version of the VDU statement, which allows the origin for any future graphics to be altered to X,Y:

VDU29,X;Y;

In the program this sets the origin for graphics to the point 640,200. This is because the function is symmetrical about X=0; so we felt the program would be clearer if the values of X ran from -640 to +640. The scaling takes place in line 60. The 800 enlarges the plot to fill most of the screen and the X/32 controls the number of bumps on the curve. Such scaling is usually best done by starting with an intelligent guess, displaying the resulting plot and then adjusting the scaling.

6.2 Activities

This activity helps you to appreciate the importance of scaling on the appearance of a display.

i. Enter the program of Listing 6.1 and run it.

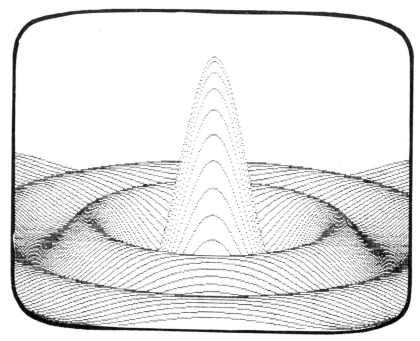

Screen Display 6.2

ii. Try altering the overall size of the display by varying the scaling factor 800 in line 60.

iii. Try altering the number of 'bumps' in the display by varying the scaling factor 32 in line 60.

iv. In line 50 the value of X is purposely set to start at -640.1 rather than at -640 exactly. Investigate why, by altering to -640.

v. Try adding STEP 4 to line 50 in order to speed things up.
_____

6.3 Drawing the surface

We now show how to use SIN(R)/R to produce the symmetrical three dimensional ripple surface of Screen Display 6.2. The height of any point on the surface is dictated by the value of the function at that point. There is a central, main 'bump' just as

```
   Listing 6.2
10 REM A program to illustrate plotting a 3D ripple
   surface
20 MODE0:VDU19,0,4;0; :REM Mode 4 for Model A
30 REM Or MODE 0 with line 110 STEP 4 and 120 STEP 16
40 REM Set up scale of picture
50 XM=640.1    :REM Size across the screen
60 ZM=800      :REM Apparent depth of view
70 YM=700      :REM Height of 'bump' on screen
80 tilt=20     :REM Angle of view
90 ST=SIN(RAD(tilt)) :CT=COS(RAD(tilt))
100 VDU 29,640;300;
110 FOR X=-XM TO 0 STEP 4
120   FOR Y=-ZM TO ZM STEP 16
130     screenY=Y*ST+CT*YM*FNsin(X,Y)
140     IF Y=-ZM THEN minY=screenY :maxY=screenY :REM
        For hidden lines
150     IF screenY>maxY THEN maxY=screenY :PROCplot
160     IF screenY<minY THEN minY=screenY :PROCplot
170   NEXT Y
180   NEXT X
190 VDU5:MOVE0,1050:END
200 :
210 DEF PROCplot
220 PLOT69,X,screenY :PLOT69,-X,screenY
230 ENDPROC
240 :
250 DEFFNsin(X,Y)
260 KR=.02*SQR(X*X+Y*Y)
270 =SIN(KR)/KR
```

there is for the two dimensional view of Screen Display 6.1.
Indeed this two dimensional view is a section through the three
dimensional one.

As you can see from Listing 6.2, the origin for all the
plotting is set centrally on the screen using the VDU29,640;300;
statement on line 100. The scale for the surface is set up in
lines 50 to 70 in terms of XM, the breadth, ZM the apparent
distance front to back and YM which scales the diagram in the
up/down direction, affecting the apparent height of the 'bumps'.

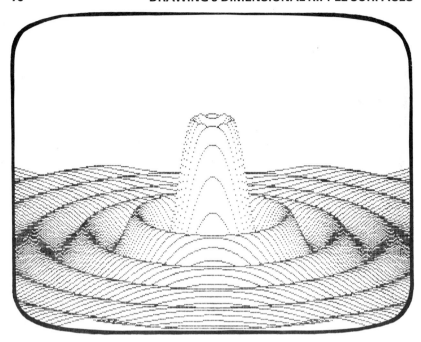

Screen Display 6.3

The value of the function SIN(KR)/KR is calculated in the function definition in lines 250 to 270. If you have your own function, you could substitute a different definition. Other functions would be equally suitable, provided that they are calculatable in terms of X and Y, although only certain types give an attractive appearance. By way of illustration, Screen Displays 6.3 and 6.4 rely on different functions. Listings 6.3 and 6.4 give the programs that produce them.

The appearance of three dimensional displays is very much improved if a line or curve is not drawn where it seems to be behind something else. In Listing 6.2, this is achieved in lines 140 to 160. However, as the process is so important in all areas of graphics, we explain in general terms in the next section.

6.4 Hidden lines

Displays of three dimensional objects invariably have some lines, which, if the surface were solid, would be hidden from sight. Where a program does not remove these lines, the whole

```
       Listing 6.3
10 REM A program to illustrate plotting a 3D ripple
      surface
20 MODE0:VDU19,0,4;0; :REM Mode 4 for Model A
30 REM Or MODE 0 with line 110 STEP 4 and 120 STEP 16
40 REM Set up scale of picture
50 XM=640.1   :REM Size across the screen
60 ZM=800     :REM Apparent depth of view
70 YM=700     :REM Height of 'bump' on screen
80 tilt=20    :REM Angle of view
90 ST=SIN(RAD(tilt)) :CT=COS(RAD(tilt))
100 VDU 29,640;300;
110 FOR X=-XM TO 0 STEP 4
120    FOR Y=-ZM TO ZM STEP 16
130      screenY=Y*ST+CT*YM*FNsin(X,Y)
140      IF Y=-ZM THEN minY=screenY :maxY=screenY :REM
         For hidden lines
150      IF screenY>maxY THEN maxY=screenY :PROCplot
160      IF screenY<minY THEN minY=screenY :PROCplot
170      NEXT Y
180    NEXT X
190 VDU5:MOVE0,1050:END
200 :
210 DEF PROCplot
220 PLOT69,X,screenY :PLOT69,-X,screenY
230 ENDPROC
240 :
250 DEFFNsin(X,Y)
260 KR=.02*SQR(X*X+Y*Y)
270 =SIN(KR)^2/KR
```

impression of solidarity is spoilt. Where the lines are removed, they are referred to as 'hidden lines'.

To remove these lines, the program draws the surface, point by point, moving from the nearest part, which must be in view, to the furthest part, which may well be hidden by something drawn earlier. While each point of the surface is being drawn, the program keeps a note of the heights up and down the screen reached so far. If the program then finds a point which lies between these two values, it must be further away, and therefore hidden from view. So it is not plotted.

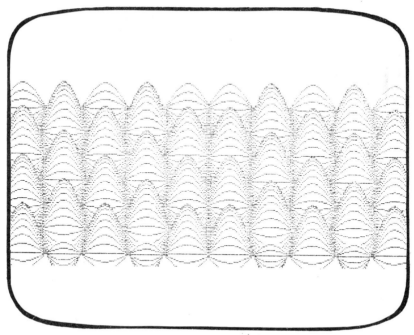

Screen Display 6.4

In Listing 6.2, the hidden line removal occurs in lines 140 to 160. Line 140 sets the starting value for the maximum and minimum height on the screen. In Lines 150 and 160 the current value is tested, to see if it lies within the range of the current maximum and minimum. If it does, the point is not plotted. If it does not, the current maximum or minimum is updated and the point is plotted.

6.5 Activities

i. Try running the three dimensional surface program using the functions which we supply.

ii. Ripple surface programs run rather slowly. How could you make the program of, for example, Listing 6.2 run more quickly? Would there be any disadvantages? (See Section 6.6.)

iii. Try producing ripple surfaces with your own functions.

```
      Listing 6.4
 10 REM A program to illustrate plotting a 3D ripple
    surface
 20 MODE0:VDU19,0,4;0; :REM Mode 4 for Model A
 30 REM Or MODE 0 with line 110 STEP 4 and 120 STEP 16
 40 REM Set up scale of picture
 50 XM=640.1    :REM Size across the screen
 60 ZM=800      :REM Apparent depth of view
 70 YM=700      :REM Height of 'bump' on screen
 80 tilt=20     :REM Angle of view
 90 ST=SIN(RAD(tilt)) :CT=COS(RAD(tilt))
100 VDU 29,640;300;
110 FOR X=-XM TO 0 STEP 4
120    FOR Y=-ZM TO ZM STEP 16
130       screenY=Y*ST+CT*YM*FNsin(X,Y)
140       IF Y=-ZM THEN minY=screenY :maxY=screenY :REM
          For hidden lines
150       IF screenY>maxY THEN maxY=screenY :PROCplot
160       IF screenY<minY THEN minY=screenY :PROCplot
170       NEXT Y
180    NEXT X
190 VDU5:MOVE0,1050:END
200 :
210 DEF PROCplot
220 PLOT69,X,screenY :PLOT69,-X,screenY
230 ENDPROC
240 :
250 DEFFNsin(X,Y)
260 KR=.02*SQR(X*X+Y*Y)
270 =0.2*SIN(X/40)*SIN(Y/80)
```

6.6 Discussion of activities

Activity 6.5ii: You can make the program run more quickly by
changing the step sizes in line 110 and line 120. You might try,
for example, 12 and 80 respectively. The resulting display is less
attractive because it is less dense.

7 Adding perspective

7.0 Introduction

You can use the graphics facilities of the BBC Microcomputer to rotate and to add perspective to objects drawn to appear in three dimensions. Screen Displays 7.1a,b,c are examples. This chapter provides and develops a suitable program (see Listing 7.1) and it explains how each part of the program works, so that you can modify it to your own requirements. In particular, the program has to take care of drawing the object, giving it perspective and rotating it. We discuss these in the next three sections.

7.1 Drawing the object

In Section 1.6, we explained one way of drawing pictures on the screen. PROCbox, for drawing rectangles, utilised co-ordinates in two-dimensions, X and Y. For the purpose of adding perspective and rotating, however, you have to work with an additional Z co-ordinate to specify how far any point is away from the screen. Only when the computer has this information can it estimate the foreshortening that perspective and rotation would produce. So, when you design your object, you have to specify three co-ordinates for the principal points. These are X, Y and Z co-ordinates. The orientations are such that the x axis is positive towards the right, the y axis is positive in the upwards direction and the z axis is positive in the direction coming out from the screen or page. Clockwise rotations are positive, looking towards the origin from a positive position along an axis. By way of illustration, Screen Displays 7.1a,b,c respectively show the same cube rotated 25 degrees about the y axis; 25 degrees about both the x and y axes; and 25 degrees about all three axes.

It is best to have the origin of co-ordinates at the centre of the screen (at addressable points 640,512) and to have the centre of the object at the origin. This is the case for the cube of Screen Displays 7.1a,b,c.

You specify the co-ordinates in any convenient units and supply a conversion factor to turn them into screen co-ordinates.

Once you have specified these, the next step is to specify which of the points have to be joined up and which not. In the program of Listing 7.1, we do this with two codes: 5 for a PLOT5,X,Y to draw to join the points and 4 to move between the two points without joining them. We use the codes after the co-ordinates of each point, in DATA statements (see lines 310 to 330). They eventually arrive as M in the PLOT statement in line 280.

7.2 Giving the object perspective

Parallel lines seem to get closer together as they get further away from the eye. This is an example of perspective, and this is the effect that our program has to achieve. It is actually very simple. The perspective scaling depends on the distance of the point from the observer, and must be such that the size of parts of the object appear smaller if they are farther away from the observer. Any part of the object sufficiently far away should tend to a zero size. If the screen co-ordinates X and Y represent projections of the image's X and Y co-ordinates, then the perspective must only depend on the Z co-ordinate. The perspective scaling can be produced by multiplying each X and Y co-ordinate by the following, where Z is the Z co-ordinate of the point and P is a length which determines the amount of perspective in the image:

$$P/(P-Z)$$

P represents the distance of the viewer's eye from the origin, i.e. from the centre of the object. It is measured in the same units as those for the size of the object. Good perspective seems to be obtained by viewing the object at a distance of about 3 times its height. This gives a perspective corresponding to viewing a book at arm's length. In Listing 7.1 the height of the cube is 2. Since we want it viewed at distance of 3 times this value, P becomes 6 (see line 140).

7.3 Rotating the object

When an object is rotated, the amount of foreshortening changes. In principle it is not very difficult to work this out in terms of the sine or cosine of the angle through which the object is rotated. However, for objects in three dimensions, the mathematics becomes very complex indeed. The best way of approaching it is via matrix algebra. We have worked out three suitable expressions for you to use: one each for lengths originally lying in the x, y and z directions. We express our results in terms of variables rather than sines and cosines. This is because it would be too time consuming for the program to keep having to evaluate the same trigonometric ratios. So the program evaluates them once only and then calls on them, as they keep being needed. These variables as are as follows:

> SX = sine of angle of rotation around x axis
> CX = cosine of angle of rotation around x axis
> SY = sine of angle of rotation around y axis
> CY = cosine of angle of rotation around y axis
> SZ = sine of angle of rotation around z axis
> CZ = cosine of angle of rotation around z axis

Our expressions for the screen co-ordinates for any point in the image are given in terms of these variables in lines 250, 260 and 270, which also includes the perspective factor. If you are familiar with matrix algebra, you should have no difficulty in deriving these expressions for yourself. If not, you will probably be prepared to accept them as we give them.

7.4 The complete program

The program starts by asking for the angles of rotation around the three axes. The next line then calculates all the sines and cosines that are required. This takes a relatively long time and so is done only once in the program. Once the mode is set in line 10, the graphics origin is fixed at the centre of the screen by the VDU29 statement in line 120. For simplicity the corners of the cube are taken to lie 1 unit along each axis, and the data for their co-ordinates are stored in the DATA statements at the end. As this means that the co-ordinates are too small for plotting directly on the screen, line 180 scales them up, according to the scaling factor K.

For programming convenience each point is plotted using a procedure called in line 190, together with the current co-ordinates and M. The procedure which does the rotation and perspective scaling is in lines 230 to 280. Line 250 calculates the Z co-ordinate first. This is then used in the next two lines to calculate the two-dimensional picture co-ordinates. The first part of the calculation of the screen co-ordinates involves the perspective scaling factor referred to in Section 7.2.

This program displays a cube which you
can view at any angle of rotation of
your choice.

When you are ready, enter the amount of
rotation required around the X, Y and Z
axes. Enter each in turn (in degrees)
separated by a comma. Then press RETURN.
0,20,0

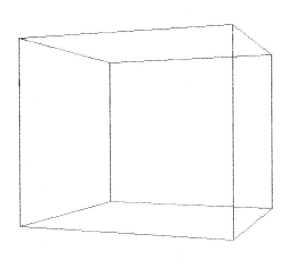

Screen Display 7.1a

This program displays a cube which you can view at any angle of rotation of your choice.

When you are ready, enter the amount of rotation required around the X, Y and Z axes. Enter each in turn (in degrees) separated by a comma. Then press RETURN.

20,20,0

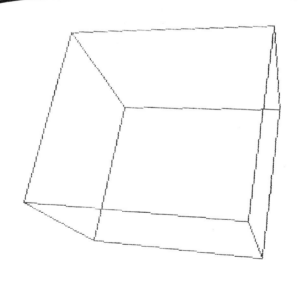

Screen Display 7.1b

This program displays a cube which you can view at any angle of rotation of your choice.

When you are ready, enter the amount of rotation required around the X, Y and Z axes. Enter each in turn (in degrees) separated by a comma. Then press RETURN.

20,20,20

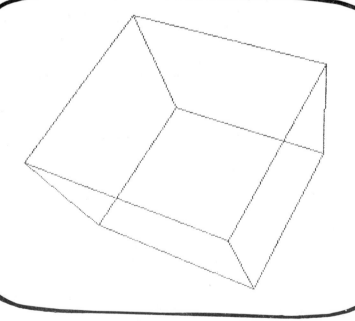

Screen Display 7.1c

Listing 7.1

```
10 MODE4:VDU19,0,4;0;19,1,3;0;
20 PRINT ' "This program displays a cube which you"
30 PRINT ' "can view at any angle of rotation of"
40 PRINT ' "your choice."
50 PRINT ' ' "When you are ready, enter the amount of"
60 PRINT ' "rotation required around the X, Y and Z"
70 PRINT ' "axes. Enter each in turn (in degrees)"
80 PRINT ' "separated by a comma. Then press RETURN."
90 INPUT ' AX,AY,AZ
100 SX=SIN(RAD(AX)):CX=COS(RAD(AX)):SY=SIN(RAD(AY))
110 CY=COS(RAD(AY)):SZ=SIN(RAD(AZ)):CZ=COS(RAD(AZ))
120 VDU29,640;512;
130 CLG
140 P=6 :K=300 :P=P*K
150 READ N
160 REPEAT
170    READ X,Y,Z,M
180    X=X*K :Y=Y*K :Z=Z*K
190    PROCplot(X,Y,Z,M)
200    N=N-1 :UNTIL N=1
210    END
220
230    DEF PROCplot(X,Y,Z,M)
240    REM X and Y are the co-ordinates M is the PLOT
       number
250    ZT=X*SY-Y*SX*CY+Z*CX*CY
260    XT=P/(P-ZT)*(X*CY*CZ+Y*(SX*SY*CZ+CX*SZ)+Z*
       (SX*SY-CX*SY*CZ))
270    YT=P/(P-ZT)*(-X*CY*SZ+Y*(CX*CZ-SX*SY*SZ)+Z*
       (SX*CZ+CX*SY*SZ))
280    PLOTM,XT,YT :ENDPROC
290
300    REM The Cartesian co-ordinates for the points
       shown in screen display 7.1
310    DATA 17,1,1,1,4, -1,1,1,5, -1,-1,1,5, 1,-1,1,5,
         1,1,1,5
320    DATA 1,1,-1,5, -1,1,-1,5, -1,-1,-1,5, 1,-1,-1,5,
         1,1,-1,5
330    DATA -1,1,1,4, -1,1,-1,5, -1,-1,1,4, -1,-1,-1,5,
         1,-1,1,4, 1,-1,-1,5
```

Degs to Rads.

K: Conversion Factor

7.5 Activities

i. Enter and run the program in Listing 7.1. Try rotating around the x axis by small angles, say between 1 and 20 degrees.

ii. Repeat for rotations around the y and the z axes.

iii. Now enter the following three lines and run the program:

```
 85 AY=25 :AZ=25
 90 FOR AX=1 TO 30 STEP 4
 95 RESTORE
205 NEXT AX
```

Does the cube rotate?

7.6 Two techniques for hidden line removal

In Section 6.4, we touched on hidden line removal. We now illustrate two methods for it - but they have to be rather simplistic because the whole subject is so complex.

Screen Displays 7.2a,b,c illustrate the simplest of the two. It shows a house and garden - and we only draw the parts of the house that can be seen from the front! In other words, we only give the co-ordinates for two sides of the complete figure! The perspective view is still perfectly acceptable, provided the house is not rotated too far around any of the axes. Even though the acceptability breaks down with larger angles, the technique is still valuable, because it gives a picture which is more pleasing and less obstructed than a wire-frame one showing all the details at the back.

You may like to experiment with another way of achieving hidden line removal (see Screen Display 7.3 and Listing 7.3). For this, you make each face of the figure a solid block of colour. The figure is then drawn starting with the areas furthest from the viewing point and working to the nearest areas. Then if any of the nearer areas, which are drawn later, cover up those already drawn, hidden line removal is automatically achieved. The technique requires rewriting the data into blocks, each representing an area. The program then needs to search through these areas and make sure that it draws them in the order of their distance from the viewing point. Our program makes no

This program demonstrates a simple
method of hidden line removal, which
only works for a small range of
orientations.

When you are ready, type the amount of
rotation required around the X, Y and Z
axes. Type each in turn (in degrees)
separated by a comma. Then press RETURN.
Rotation Angles?-5,12,0

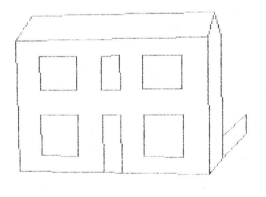

Screen Display 7.2a

This program demonstrates a simple
method of hidden line removal, which
only works for a small range of
orientations.

When you are ready, type the amount of
rotation required around the X, Y and Z
axes. Type each in turn (in degrees)
separated by a comma. Then press RETURN.
Rotation Angles?-10,15,0

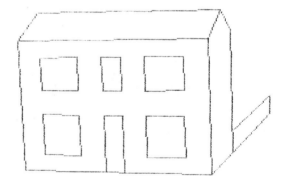

Screen Display 7.2b

This program demonstrates a simple
method of hidden line removal, which
only works for a small range of
orientations.

When you are ready, type the amount of
rotation required around the X, Y and Z
axes. Type each in turn (in degrees)
separated by a comma. Then press RETURN.
Rotation Angles?-10,30,0

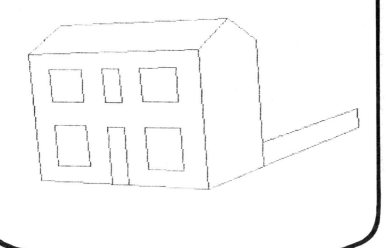

Screen Display 7.2c

Listing 7.2

```
 10 MODE4:VDU19,0,4;0;19,1,3;0;
 20 PRINT ' "This program demonstrates a simple"
 30 PRINT ' "method of hidden line removal, which"
 40 PRINT ' "only works for a small range of"
 50 PRINT ' "orientations."
 60 PRINT ' ' "When you are ready, type the amount of"
 70 PRINT ' "rotation required around the X, Y and Z"
 80 PRINT ' "axes. Type each in turn (in degrees)"
 90 PRINT ' "separated by a comma. Then press RETURN."
100 INPUT ' "Rotation Angles",AX,AY,AZ
110 SX=SIN(RAD(AX)):CX=COS(RAD(AX)):SY=SIN(RAD(AY))
120 CY=COS(RAD(AY)):SZ=SIN(RAD(AZ)):CZ=COS(RAD(AZ))
130 VDU29,400;500;
140 CLS
150 K=6 :P=500
160 RESTORE
170 READ N
180 FOR I=1 TO N
190    READ X,Y,Z,M
200    PROCplot(X,Y,Z,M)
210    NEXT I
220 END
230
240 DEF PROCplot(X,Y,Z,M)
250 REM X and Y are the co-ordinates M is the PLOT
    number
260 ZT=X*SY-Y*SX*CY+Z*CX*CY
270 XT=P/(P-ZT)*(X*CY*CZ+Y*(SX*SY*CZ+CX*SZ)+Z*
    (SX*SY-CX*SY*CZ))
280 YT=P/(P-ZT)*(-X*CY*SZ+Y*(CX*CZ-SX*SY*SZ)+Z*
    (SX*CZ+CX*SY*SZ))
290 PLOTM,K*XT,K*YT :ENDPROC
300
310 DATA 46
320 DATA -50,-40,0,4, 50,-40,0,5, 50,40,0,5, -50,40,0,
    5, -50,-40,0,5
330 DATA -5,-40,0,4, -5,-5,0,5, 5,-5,0,5, 5,-40,0,5
340 DATA -38,-30,0,4, -18,-30,0,5, -18,-5,0,5, -38,-5,
    0,5, -38,-30,0,5
350 DATA 17,-30,0,4, 37,-30,0,5, 37,-5,0,5, 17,-5,0,5,
    17,-30,0,5
```

P.T.O.

```
Listing 7.2  continued
360 DATA -38,10,0,4, -18,10,0,5, -18,30,0,5, -38,30,0,
    5, -38,10,0,5
370 DATA 17,10,0,4, 37,10,0,5, 37,30,0,5, 17,30,0,5, 1
    7,10,0,5
380 DATA -5,10,0,4, 5,10,0,5, 5,30,0,5, -5,30,0,5,
    -5,10,0,5
390 DATA 50,-40,0,4, 50,-40,-60,5, 50,40,-60,5,
    50,55,-30,5, 50,40,0,5
400 DATA 50,-40,-60,4, 50,-40,-200,5, 50,-25,-200,5,
    50,-25,-60,5
410 DATA 50,55,-30,4, -50,55,-30,5, -50,40,0,5
```

attempt at such a search but merely draws the faces of the cube in a fixed order. This means that if the cube is rotated too far the illusion is spoilt.

7.7 Activities

i. Enter the house and garden program of Listing 7.2 and experiment with the rotations to examine the limitations of such a partial model.

ii. Run the program of Listing 7.2. How do you feel about the way it removes hidden lines?

iii. Run the program of Listing 7.3. How do you feel about the way it removes hidden lines?

This program displays a cube which you
can view at any angle of rotation of
your choice.

When you are ready, enter the amount of
rotation required around the X, Y and Z
axes. Enter each in turn (in degrees)
separated by a comma. Then press RETURN.
-20,20,0

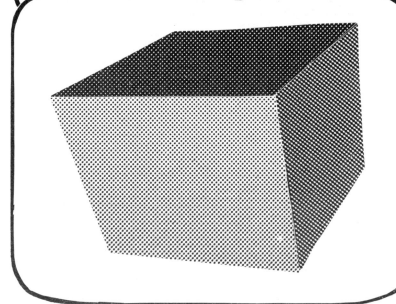

Screen Display 7.3

```
    Listing 7.3
10 MODE4:VDU19,0,4;0;19,1,3;0;
20 PRINT ' "This program displays a cube which you"
30 PRINT ' "can view at any angle of rotation of"
40 PRINT ' "your choice."
50 PRINT ' ' "When you are ready, enter the amount of"
60 PRINT ' "rotation required around the X, Y and Z"
70 PRINT ' "axes. Enter each in turn (in degrees)"
80 PRINT ' "separated by a comma. Then press RETURN."
90 INPUT ' AX,AY,AZ
100 MODE2 :REM Mode 5 for a Model A
110 SX=SIN(RAD(AX)):CX=COS(RAD(AX)):SY=SIN(RAD(AY)):
    CY=COS(RAD(AY)):SZ=SIN(RAD(AZ)):CZ=COS(RAD(AZ))
120 VDU29,640;512;
130 P=6 :K=300 :P=P*K
140 READ N
150 REPEAT
160    READ X,Y,Z,M,C
170    GCOL0,C
180    X=X*K:Y=Y*K:Z=Z*K
190    PROCplot(X,Y,Z,M)
200    N=N-1 :UNTIL N=1
210 END
220
230 DEF PROCplot(X,Y,Z,M)
240 REM X and Y are the co-ordinates M is the
    PLOT number
250 ZT=X*SY-Y*SX*CY+Z*CX*CY
260 XT=P/(P-ZT) * (X*CY*CZ+Y* (SX*SY*CZ+CX*SZ) +Z*
    (SX*SY-CX*SY*CZ))
270 YT=P/(P-ZT) * (-X*CY*SZ+Y* (CX*CZ-SX*SY*SZ) +Z*
    (SX*CZ+CX*SY*SZ))
280 PLOTM,XT,YT :ENDPROC
290
300 REM e.g. The Cartesian coordinates for points
    shown in fig 7-3
310 DATA19
320 DATA 1,1,-1,4,1, -1,1,-1,4,1, 1,-1,-1,85,1,
    -1,-1,-1,85,1
330 DATA 1,-1,1,4,2, 1,-1,-1,4,2, -1,-1,1,85,2,
    -1,-1,-1,85,2
340 DATA -1,1,1,85,3, -1,1,-1,85,3
350 DATA 1,1,1,85,4, 1,1,-1,85,4
360 DATA 1,-1,1,85,5, 1,-1,-1,85,5
370 DATA 1,1,1,4,6, -1,1,1,4,6,
    1,-1,1,85,6, -1,-1,1,85,6
```

8 Extending BBC BASIC for graphics

8.0 Introduction

We have now explained enough about the graphics facilities of the BBC Microcomputer for you to be able to program your own very elegant graphics displays. Nevertheless, if you were to try using these graphics facilities seriously, you would still find yourself putting in a great deal of time and effort. So we have done something which we regard as a special feature of this book - something which simplifies the programming for you and removes all the drudgery. In consequence, you become free to concentrate on designing the display that you want, with little thought to the programming. We hope and believe that you will produce better displays as a result.

The special feature is that we provide routines which perform all the essential, mundane parts of graphics for you. All you have to do is to type them in from Appendix 1 and save them ready to include them in programs as you require them. Or, if you prefer, you can buy them ready-recorded on a cassette. Because of how they are recorded, there is no problem with transferring them to disk. There are two advantages to buying them ready-recorded. Firstly, it saves you the effort of typing; and secondly you will not have the frustration of searching out the typing errors that you, like everyone else, will inevitably make.

In effect, our routines provide a sophisticated extension of BBC BASIC. Firstly, like BBC BASIC, they are instantly available - you merely call on them as procedures. Secondly, just as you do not need to know how the computer achieves such things as printing and listing from the PRINT and LIST instructions of BBC BASIC, neither do you need to know how our routines work - although we do explain in Appendix 2, in case you are interested. The essential thing is that you should know how to use the procedures.

This chapter is concerned with introducing you to the procedures. We tell you what they can do, and illustrate with some of the simpler ones. You will see that you need very little programming expertise to use them.

The displays in all the following chapters rely heavily on our procedures. In order to use most of them, you will have to be able to feed data into a program and store it as arrays. We also discuss this later in the chapter.

8.1 Our procedures

We provide our routines as procedures which we believe that you will need to call over and over again in graphics programming. A complete list is in Appendix 1, and Appendix 2 explains how each one works.

We shall be saying more about these procedures as we come to them in the rest of the book. In the next section we illustrate the use of three of them.

8.2 Procedures for enlarged, rotated writing

Any graphics display is livened up with enlarged writing, set at an angle or going round a circle. Using our procedures, you can produce it for yourself, either character by character or as a complete message. It can be in a straight line or round the arc of a circle. You do not have to understand details of the programming. You merely have to call on one of three procedures: PROCmessage, PROCchr and PROCcurve.

These procedures are expressed in terms of:

S$ which is the string holding whatever is
         to be printed.

X, Y   which are the normal screen co-ordinates.
         They are in the range 0 - 1279 for X and
         1023 for Y.

SC   which is a scaling factor for whatever is
         to be printed. You select its magnitude
         through trial and error.

AN, SA and FA which are angles in radians. Zero
         is straight up, and anti-clockwise is the
         positive direction.

R   which is the radius of a circle in screen
         units around which text is printed.

The procedures have to be used in a graphics mode. This is what they do:

PROCchr(X,Y,S$,AN,SC) prints the single character held in S$ with the lower left-hand corner of the character at the position X,Y.

PROCmessage(X,Y,S$,AN,SC) prints the message held in S$, starting at the position X,Y.

PROCcurve(X,Y,R,SA,FA,S$,SC) prints the message held in S$, round the arc of a circle of radius R, starting at the position X,Y.

8.3 Using the procedures for large, rotated writing

Once you have the appropriate procedures in memory, you can either call on them within a program or using the direct mode.

PROCmessage(600,0,"Straight up",0,10)

Figure 8.1. The result of a call to PROCmessage.

For example, Figure 8.1 shows the result of a call to PROCmessage in the following program:

```
10 MODE 4
20 PROCmessage(640,0,"straight up",0,10)
30 END
```

Line 10 gives the co-ordinate for the start of the message as the bottom of the screen (640,0). The angle is zero for straight up and the magnification is 10.

Figure 8.2, a message for all Australians, shows the result of the following call to PROCmessage in the direct mode:

PROCmessage(1200,540,"Wrong way up pommy",PI/2,8)

This message starts at the position 1200,540; the angle is exactly half of PI to give a quarter of a turn to the left, making the message upside-down. The scaling factor is 8.

Ꭱwwod dn Ꭱem 6uoᴚₘ

PROCmessage(1200,540,"Wrong way up pommy",PI/2,8)

Figure 8.2. The result of a call to PROCmessage.

PROCmessage(600,950,"Down",PI,30)

Figure 8.3. The result of a call to PROCmessage.

A message printed straight down the screen requires AN to be PI, as shown in Figure 8.3. It is produced by the following line:

PROCmessage(640,1023,"down",PI,30)

A message printed across the screen diagonally from top left to bottom right is shown in Figure 8.4 and is produced by the following, where the co-ordinates of the top left-hand side of the 'd' are 60,920, the angle of the writing is just over PI for just over a half turn anticlockwise and SC is 20:

PROCmessage(60,920,"diagonal",PI*1.3,20)

PROCmessage(60,920,"diagonal",PI*1.3,20)

Figure 8.4. The result of a call to PROCmessage.

Screen Display 8.1 is a display along two curves, one bowing downwards from the top two corners and the other coming up from the bottom two corners. It shows the title of this book and our names, and is produced by the program of Listing 8.1.

8.4 Activities

Put the procedures PROCmessage, PROCchr and PROCcurve into memory. Either you can type them in from the listings in Appendix 1 and save them on cassette tape using the *EXEC format as described in Section 0.2, or you can use the ready-recorded cassette, which is available for purchase. We shall refer to the composite listing of these three procedures as TEXT.

i. Now use our procedures, as explained in the previous section, to write your name across the corners of the screen. You will need to experiment to get the writing in the right place and of a suitable size.

ii. Write a program to write out your name continuously along a sine wave. We give one possibility in Section 8.9.

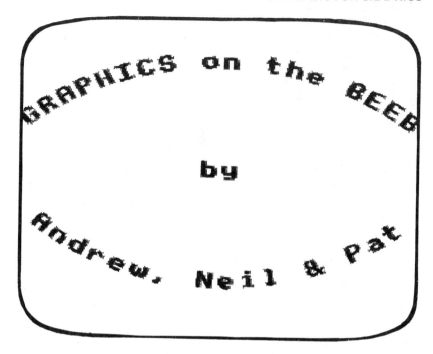

Screen Display 8.1

8.5 Feeding data into programs

Our other procedures, which form the backbone of the rest of the book, help to display information in various ways, for example as graphs, pie charts and histograms. This information has to be already available within the program for the procedure to use and you have to be able to put it in.

There are several ways of feeding data into programs, and we illustrate most of them in the rest of the book. At this stage, however, it is worth saying a few words about two: DATA statements and INPUT statements.

The INPUT statement allows you or any other user of the program to feed in data, while the program is running, in response to requests appearing on the screen. This dialogue between the user and the computer has the advantage of being user-friendly. So we shall use INPUT statements quite frequently.

```
      Listing 8.1
10 MODE4
20 XB=100:YB=180:AN=PI/8
30 SC=8
40 M$=" GRAPHICS on the BEEB"
50 PROCcurve(640,0,900,PI*.25,-PI*.251,M$,SC)
60 PROCmessage(578,512,"by",PI*1.5,8)
70 M$=" Andrew, Neil & Pat"
80 PROCcurve(640,1024,900,PI*.75,PI*1.25,M$,-SC)
90 :
100 END
```

When we demonstrate the programs relying on our procedures, we shall show the resulting dialogue as part of the screen display, and we shall underline everything that the user puts in, so as to distinguish it from the printout produced by the program.

DATA statements are better for feeding in data when you want to store the resulting display. You can feed in the data, look at the display and then experiment with the data to improve the display by editing the DATA statements. The editing facilities of the BBC Microcomputer are excellent for this purpose.

8.6 Storing data: arrays

Normally, all the data which our procedures require have to be taken from arrays - and your program must set them up. Since the procedures are concerned with graphical data, which normally consists of two co-ordinates, two arrays are generally required: arrays X() and Y(). They can store any number of items. X(0) holds the number of the co-ordinates, ie the number of values stored in either X() or Y(). Suppose, for the sake of illustration, that there are to be 20 co-ordinates. Then the following is a suitable program line to define the arrays:

    10 DIM X(20),Y(20)

You can store data in the arrays by any of the following statements:

50 X(I)=5 :Y(I)=4.8

or

50 X(I)=n :Y(I)=m

or

50 READ X(I),YI()

or

50 INPUT #A,X(I),Y(I)

or

50 INPUT "next values ",X(I),Y(I) etc.

The variable I could be replaced by a number, although a variable is more likely in such a situation.

When all of the values have been stored in the arrays and before any of the procedures are called, you must place the number of stored data pairs into X(0) by a line such as:

160 X(0)=I

or

160 X(0)=18 etc.

The following is a rather facile example of a minimum set of lines that would be required before any of our procedures are called:

10 DIM X(2),Y(2)
20 MODE 4
30 X(1)=1 :Y(1)=1
40 X(2)=3 :Y(2)=5
50 X(0)=2

Line 10 dimensions the array to set enough storage space aside for the number of values your program requires. As none of the procedures set the graphics mode, you must do this yourself in the program, and this is the purpose of line 20. Such a line is essential before any plotting. Otherwise the program remains in mode 7 and no graphics appears on the screen! Lines 30 and 40 merely place some co-ordinates into the arrays, while line 50 records the number of values stored in the array.

8.7 The core procedures

Although we have quite a sizeable collection of procedures, a few form the backbone of the graphics in the rest of the book. We refer to them as the core procedures. They are:

- PROCscale
- PROCaxes
- PROCgraduate
- PROCnumber
- PROCpoint
- PROCgraph
- PROCnamex
- PROCnamey
- PROCbstln

This is what these procedures do:

PROCscale scales your graphics for you, ensuring that the data that you supply always fits nicely onto the screen. This frees you from having to consider screen co-ordinates and addressable points, etc.

PROCaxes draws a pair of axes i.e. an x axis and a y axis. The axes do not necessarily cross at the origin, because PROCscale examines the range of the values supplied to it and accordingly sets where the axes should cross in order to make the best display. (Incidentally an axis always starts from zero if the smallest inputted co-ordinate is less than 1/3 of the largest - although we show later how this can be altered.)

PROCgraduate marks off the axes into appropriate intervals: never less that three or more than 30 graduations along each axis. To make it easier to read values from the graphs, every fifth graduation is larger than the rest.

PROCnumber prints a number against the first and last scale division for each axis to indicate the scale.

PROCpoint marks a single + at the point specified when the procedure is called.

PROCgraph combines the above procedures, i.e. it causes a pair of suitably scaled, graduated and numbered axes to be plotted.

PROCnamex names the x axis by printing whatever wording you want along the x axis.

PROCnamey names the y axis by printing whatever wording you want along the y axis. You call PROCnamex and PROCnamey with lines like the following, which must include the words that you want printed:

```
100 PROCnamex("the x axis")
110 PROCnamey("the y axis")
```

PROCbstln draws the best straight line through a set of points whose co-ordinates you supply.

We advise you make sure, now, that these core procedures are available for you to use. You can either type them into the computer from Appendix 1 and save them, or you can buy the ready-recorded tape. We shall refer to the composite listing of these procedures as COMP (to stand for composite). If you have a Model A and get a 'Bad MODE' error message, it means that you do not have enough memory space for all our procedures. Nevertheless a Model A does not stop you from getting meaningful displays! You can normally still get them, as long as you do not mind missing out on such things as numbering, graduating and labelling the axes. You merely have to delete the lines of the less-important procedures (PROCnumber, PROCgraduate, PROCnamex and PROCnamey) and all references to them. You should also delete PROCbstln and all but the most essential lines in your program.

The following activities give an introduction to what the core procedures can do - although we elaborate and extend in the rest of the book.

8.8 Activities

If you have not already done so, record at least PROCaxes, PROCgraduate, PROCnumber and PROCpoint using the *EXEC format as described in Section 0.2. We shall refer to this as COMP to stand for 'composite'. (If you have a Model A, there is only memory space for PROCscale and PROCaxis.)

i. Enter the following short program to call on PROCscale. Add all the procedures using the command *EXEC "COMP" and run the program, thereby activating the other graphics procedures:

```
10 MODE 4
20 DIM X(2),Y(2)
30 X(1)=1 :Y(1)=1
40 X(2)=3 :Y(2)=3
50 X(0)=2
60 PROCscale
70 END
```

ii. We shall shortly be asking you to call on some of our procedures in the direct mode. In order to keep this apart from the resulting display, first enter the following, where VDU 28 defines a window in which text is confined:

```
CLS:VDU 28,10,2,30,0
```

Now enter the following in direct mode, so that you can see its effect:

```
PROCaxes
```

iii. Repeat with each of the following procedures in turn.

```
PROCgraduate
PROCnumber
PROCpoint(2,2)
PROCpoint(3,3)
```

Do you see that each axis has a scale running from 1 to 3, with larger divisions for 1, 1.5, 2, 2.5 and 3? This makes it easier to read values from the graph.

iv. Repeat with the following:

```
PROCpoint(-1,-1)
```

Why does this seem to have no effect? We discuss this in Section 8.9.

v. Now change line 30 in the above program to:

```
30 X(1)=.9 :Y(1)=.9
```

Run the program again, followed by the direct mode procedure calls. Note the new scales for the axes, which both now run from zero.

8.9 Discussion of activities

Activity 8.4 ii: Our program for writing your name continuously along a sine wave is given below:

```
10 MODE4
20 INPUT"Enter your name",A$
30 CLS
40 A$=A$+"  "
```

```
 50 P=0
 60 FOR A=0 TO 2*PI STEP PI/10
 70    P=P+1 :IF P>LEN(A$) THEN P=1
 80    PROCchr(A*200,512+400*SIN(A),MID$(A$,P,1),0,10)
 90    NEXT A
100 END
```

Activity 8.8 iv: PROCpoint(-1,-1) gives a point off the graph because the point is outside the range given in the call to PROCscale.

9 Drawing graphs

9.0 Introduction

It is always useful to be able to display information graphically. Graphs are more visually attractive than print. They get information across more quickly and easily, and they make it much easier to see trends. This chapter shows how to draw graphs to display your own information. It relies on the procedures which we have developed and which we assume that you have now recorded: either by typing them in from Appendix 1

or as the ready-recorded tape. These procedures free you from
having to worry about programming such things as a suitable
range for the graph; scaling it to fit onto the screen; and
drawing, marking and labelling the axes. Your only concern will
be to program some lines to act as a 'driver' for our procedures -
and we now go on to explain how to do this.

We shall illustrate three ways of feeding in data: getting the
computer to calculate the data from a formula, plus some
starting conditions; providing the data, as co-ordinates for each of
the points to be plotted; and from data entered at the time the
program is run.

9.1 Data calculated by the program

In this section we illustrate drawing a graph which gets the
computer to calculate the data from a formula and some starting
conditions. Our example is a graph to show the mortgage still
owing on a house as a function of year (see Screen Display 9.1).
The program is given in Listing 9.1. Apart from the lines which
define the procedure PROCgraph, and line 170 which we explain
in the next section, the program is probably self-explanatory. Line
10 sets the foreground and background colours. Then the program
is concerned with calculating values to fill two arrays which hold
the co-ordinates of the points to be plotted on the graph. We
decided, quite arbitrarily, to have 20 points on the graph. So we
dimensioned the arrays X() and Y() to 20 in line 50 and we set
the limit of the REPEAT...UNTIL loop to 'year' > 19 in line 110.
Lines 80 to 100 perform a calculation of the mortgage still
owing, assuming a starting capital of 10000 with an annual
interest rate of 13.5%. Once the program has written the values
of the co-ordinates of the points to be plotted into the arrays X()
and Y(), and once X(0) has been given the number of the points,
line 140 calls PROCgraph. This itself calls on other procedures. It
consequently takes care of scaling the display to fit the screen,
drawing, graduating and numbering the axes and plotting the
points.

We hope and expect that, armed with this example, you will
be able to draw graphs to display data of your own. When you
come to do so, it may be worth bearing the following points in
mind. Firstly there are other ways of filling the arrays X() and
Y(), and some may be more suitable than others for your purpose.
Secondly PROCgraph has to be called by a line such as:

        100 PROCgraph

It expects to find arrays X() and Y() which must have previously been dimensioned with a line such as:

    10 DIM X(20),Y(20)

where:

        20 is the number of points to be plotted,
        X(0) = number of points
        X(1), X(2), etc are the x co-ordinates of points to be plotted
        Y(1), Y(2), etc are the corresponding y co-ordinates.

9.2 Removal of the cursor from the final display

Since the existence of the cursor tends to spoil any graphical display, the program of Listing 9.1 removes it to outside the screen area once the graph is complete. It uses a VDU statement to define that text should be written at the graphics cursor. Then the graphics, and therefore the cursor, are moved off the screen. Both operations are performed by the single line 170:

        170 VDU5 :MOVE 0,1050 :END

9.3 Activities

_____

i. Run the program of Listing 9.1. Does it behave as you expect?

ii. Now modify the program of Listing 9.1. Try changing such things as the numbers of points, the rate of interest, the number of years for repayment or the original mortage.

iii. There are many examples of graphs for which data can be calculated by the program. We hope that you will be able to use our approach to produce a graph that is particularly useful for you in some way.

_____

9.4 Data read from DATA statements

In this section we show how to draw a graph for which you supply the co-ordinates of the points directly, in DATA statements. Our example is a graph to show the variation of the air temperature (in degrees Centigrade) according to time of day

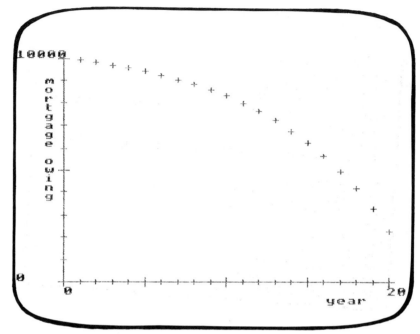

Screen Display 9.1

(in hours) on 6th August 1982 (see Screen Display 9.2). The program is given in Listing 9.2.

   The program works in the following way. The data is stored as a list of pairs of corresponding temperatures and times in the DATA statements. The number of pairs of points is the first item of data. In line 30, the first item is read in. Then the X() and Y() arrays are dimensioned and the rest of the points read in. A single call to PROCgraph in line 110 takes care of things like scaling. In essence this procedure expects the x and y values for all the points to be available for it in the arrays X() and Y(). The number of points to be plotted must be held in X(0). The program draws the axes, graduates the axes and prints up the numerical value corresponding to the ends of the axes. It plots the points with an appropriate scaling factor. This means that virtually whatever the range of the values supplied as the co-ordinates for the points, they are suitably scaled for display. The colours for the foreground and background are set in line 10.

   You can easily modify this program to display your own data. You keep most of the program as it is and only have to modify

```
    Listing 9.1
10 MODE4:VDU19,1,3;0;19,0,4;0;
20 mortgage=10000
30 interestrate=13.5
40 monthpayments=120
50 DIM X(20),Y(20)   :REM X()=year count, Y()=mortgage
60 year=0
70 REPEAT
80    mortgage=mortgage+interestrate*mortgage/100-12*
      monthpayments
90    year=year+1
100   X(year)=year :Y(year)=mortgage
110   UNTIL year>19 OR mortgage<0
120
130 X(0)=year
140 PROCgraph
150 PROCnamex("year")
160 PROCnamey("mortgage owing")
170 VDU5 :MOVE 0,1050 :END
```

lines 130 and 140 which label the axes, and the data in the
DATA statements. It is best to put the DATA statements at the
end of the program. This has the advantage that you can enter
the data, then check and alter as necessary using the BBC
Microcomputer's excellent editing facilities. For example, we give
16 as the number of pairs of points in the first item of data in
line 170, but you can of course choose to have a different
number of pairs of points.

9.5 Titles and other labels

You probably noticed that the title of the graph of Screen
Display 9.2 is written with the line:

   120 PRINT TAB(8,2);"AIR TEMPERATURE ON 6th AUGUST"

This method of writing relies on the use of the TAB function in
a PRINT statement. The first value in the TAB function provides
the character position along the line at which printing should

```
This program will display the points

which you provide as co-ordinates, a

pair at a time. When you are asked for

the co-ordinates of each point, please

type the X co-ordinate first, then a

comma, then the Y co-ordinate. Then

press RETURN.


How many points do you want ?10
Co-ordinates of point 1?1974,100
Co-ordinates of point 2?1975,100
Co-ordinates of point 3?1976,101
Co-ordinates of point 4?1977,101
Co-ordinates of point 5?1978,102
Co-ordinates of point 6?1979,102
Co-ordinates of point 7?1980,1031981,
Co-ordinates of point 8?1981,104
Co-ordinates of point 9?1982,106
Co-ordinates of point 10?1983,110
```

Screen Display 9.2 (first part)

start, the first character position being zero. The second gives
the line number, counting the first line at the top of the screen
as zero.

This method of writing can also be useful for labelling the
axes. You may like to experiment with it, as an alternative to
PROCnamex and PROCnamey. It always writes horizontally,
whereas PROCnamex and PROCnamey write along the axes.

You can also label graphs using PROCchr or PROCmessage,
as explained in Chapter 8. The large writing is particularly
suitable for titles.

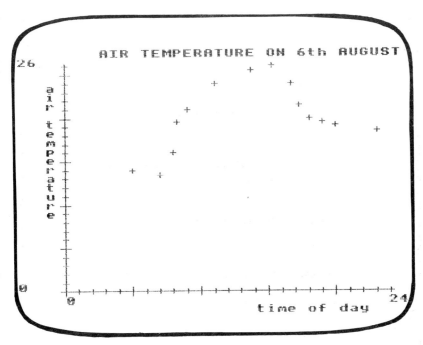

Screen Display 9.2. (second part)

9.6 Activities

i. Run the program of Listing 9.2. Does it behave as you expect?

ii. Try using the TAB function method, instead of PROCnamex and PROCnamey, to label the axes. Which method of naming axes do you prefer? While experimenting with naming the axes, you may like to try upper case letters and then lower case letters. Graphics artists often feel passionately about which looks better in which situation. Do you feel as strongly?

iii. Try using PROCchr or PROCmessage to give the display a title.

iv. Try altering the data in the DATA statements to modify the display.

```
    Listing 9.2
10 MODE 4 :VDU19,1,3;0;19,0,4;0;
20 DIM X(20),Y(20)
30 READ end
40 X(0)=end
50 N=0
60 REPEAT
70    N=N+1 :READ X(N),Y(N)
80    UNTIL N=end
90
100 CLG
110 PROCgraph
120 PRINT TAB(8,2);"AIR TEMPERATURE ON 6th AUGUST"
130 PROCnamey("air temperature")
140 PROCnamex("time of day")
150 VDU5 :MOVE0,1100 :END
160
170 DATA 16,0,0,24,0,5,14,7,13.5,8,16,8.25,19.5,9,21,
    11,24,13.75,25.6
180 DATA 15.25,26,16.75,24,17.25,21.5,18,20,19,19.5,
    20,19.2,23,18.5
```

9.7 Data taken from the INPUT statement

Our next example is a graph showing how some 'doom statistic' such as 'population' or 'energy consumption' is increasing with time, and the data is fed in using INPUT statements. This produces the rather friendly-looking dialogue between the computer and the user, and it is shown at the beginning of Screen Display 9.3a. The rest of the screen display shows what happens when a user feeds in the data which is underlined. This underlining distinguishes what the user types in from what is produced by the program of Listing 9.3a.

The program is essentially very simple. It starts in line 10 by setting the foreground and background colours. Then in line 90, it asks the user how many points are to be displayed. When this is known, the arrays are dimensioned and the co-ordinates of the points requested by line 120. PROCgraph is then called in line 180 to draw the graph.

This program will display the points

which you provide as co-ordinates, a

pair at a time. When you are asked for

the co-ordinates of each point, please

type the X co-ordinate first, then a

comma, then the Y co-ordinate. Then

press RETURN.

```
How many points do you want ?11
Co-ordinates of point 1?1974,0
Co-ordinates of point 2?1974,100
Co-ordinates of point 3?1975,100
Co-ordinates of point 4?1976,101
Co-ordinates of point 5?1977,101
Co-ordinates of point 6?1978,102
Co-ordinates of point 7?1979,102
Co-ordinates of point 8?1980,103
Co-ordinates of point 9?1981,104
Co-ordinates of point 10?1982,106
Co-ordinates of point 11?1983,110
```

Screen Display 9.3a (first part)

9.8 Forcing the inclusion of the origin

Screen Displays 9.3a and 9.3b both show graphs of how some
'doom statistic' such as 'population' or 'energy consumption' is
increasing with time. They both display the same data, but Screen
Display 9.3b does not include the origin of the y axis, whereas
Screen Display 9.3a does. The impacts of the two displays are
quite different. Screen Display 9.3a does indeed seem to support
the fact that doom is imminent, whereas Screen Display 9.3b
suggests that the 'doom statistic' is changing very little.

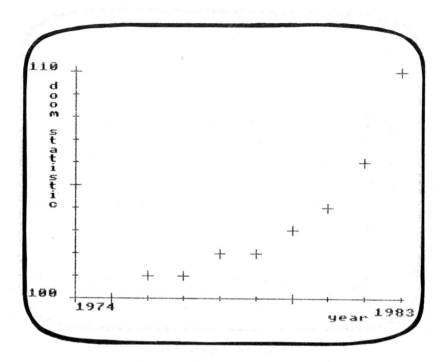

Screen Display 9.3a (second part)

So for some purposes it is can be very important that one or both axes start from zero, whereas for other purposes, it can be just as important that they do not.

The simplest way to force the inclusion of the origin is to put in one extra point which is the origin itself. This was done for Screen Display 9.3b, as you can see from the initial dialogue, where the co-ordinates of point 1, input as 1974,0, are underlined.

9.9 Activities

i. Modify the program of Listing 9.2 to include the origin on the graph of the variation of temperature with time of day.

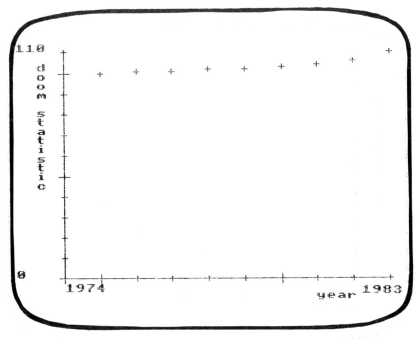

Screen Display 9.3b

ii. It is very simple indeed to modify Listing 9.3 to make it
suitable for displaying something other than a 'doom statistic'.
Modify lines 190 and 200 so that the labelling of the axes is
appropriate for displaying other data of your choice.

```
    Listing 9.3
 10 MODE4:VDU19,1,3;0;19,0,4;0;
 20 PRINT ' "This program will display the points"
 30 PRINT ' "which you provide as co-ordinates, a"
 40 PRINT ' "point at a time. When you are asked for"
 50 PRINT ' "the co-ordinates of each point, please"
 60 PRINT ' "type the X co-ordinate first, then a"
 70 PRINT ' "comma, then the Y co-ordinate. Then"
 80 PRINT ' "press RETURN."
 90 INPUT ' ' ' "How many points do you want ",N
100 DIM X(N),Y(N)
110 FOR I=1 TO N
120     PRINT ' "Co-ordinates of point ";I;
130     INPUT X(I),Y(I)
140     NEXT I
150 X(0)=N
160 CLG
170
180 PROCgraph
190 PROCnamex("label for x axis") :REM Or alternative
        label
200 PROCnamey("label for y axis") :REM Or alternative
        label
210 VDU5 :MOVE 0,1200 :END
```

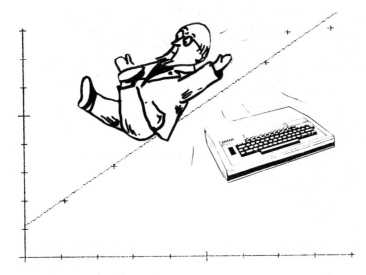

10 Getting the best straight line

10.0 Introduction

It is often useful to plot points in such a way that they lie on a straight line. There are several reasons for this. For example, any misfits are obvious at a glance. Also it is easy to make predictions from a straight line: the line can be extended (or extrapolated) beyond the range of the measurements, and in-between values can be inserted (or interpolated).

When the points that you want to plot lie very close to a straight line, it is not difficult to draw the line. The problem comes when the points are scattered widely to either side of the line. Then it is difficult to decide on the most appropriate orientation of the line. In this chapter we help by providing a procedure PROCbstln and showing how to use it.

As the next sections explain, PROCbstln does not only draw the best straight line through a set of points. It also prints up other relevant information.

10.1 The equation of a straight line

In practice PROCbstln does more than merely drawing the best straight line through any set of points which you provide. It also prints up the equation of that line. This is always in the following form, where m is the slope of the graph and c is the intercept on the Y axis:

$$Y = mX + c$$

The slope is positive if the line slopes from bottom left to top right and negative if the line slopes from top left to bottom right. The intercept on the Y axis is positive if the line cuts the Y axis above the X axis and negative if the line cuts the Y axis below the X axis.

10.2 The correlation coefficient

PROCbstln does not only print up the equation of the best straight line. It also indicates how well the points fit a straight line. It expresses this as the 'correlation coefficient'. The magnitude of a correlation coefficient can be between 0 and 1, i.e. 1 if the fit is perfect and is 0 if the fit is non-existent. The sign of a correlation coefficient indicates which way the line slopes. Bottom left to top right is positive and top left to bottom right is negative.

10.3 Using PROCbstln

In order to use PROCbstln, all you have to do is to develop some 'driver' lines and feed in your data. We shall illustrate with some data about how the total fuel consumption of a car varies with total mileage. From the point of view of the owner of the car, this is the sort of relationship that is worth plotting, because it should be more or less a straight line: the greater the mileage, the correspondingly greater the fuel consumed. Any variation from a straight line suggests that the car is not working as efficiently as it might; and the magnitude of the slope gives the average fuel consumption in miles per litre.

Screen Display 10.1 shows a graph of the mileometer reading for a car against the number of litres of petrol put into it. Listing 10.1 gives the program. You see that the data is fed in and stored as data statements. Ours was originally taken from a log book: The mileometer reading was recorded each time the car was filled with petrol, as was the amount of petrol left in the tank at the time of filling.

The program of Listing 10.1 is probably self-explanatory. It sets the foreground and background colours for the display and it uses PROCgraph, PROCnamex and PROCnamey, as explained in Chapter 8. It expects the first item in the data to be the number of sets of entries to follow. The arrays $X(n)$ and $Y(n)$ are then dimensioned. Each set of data in the data list corresponds to the figures collected each time the car is filled with petrol i.e. the mileometer reading, the petrol put in and an estimate of how much petrol was still in the tank at the time. As the petrol placed in the tank at any one filling is for miles still to be travelled, while the mileometer reading is for miles already travelled, the data for the arrays $X(n)$ and $Y(n)$ have to be read out of step, as you can see in line 50. Line 60 then sums the total petrol put in the tank, while line 70 compensates for any petrol still left in the tank. Errors in these measurements do not accumulate and, if necessary, the estimate for the fuel left in the tank when filling up can be kept at zero. This would give more scatter to the points on the graph, but the overall slope should give the same fuel consumption.

10.4 Activities

---

i. Run the program of Listing 10.1 and see if it behaves as you expect.

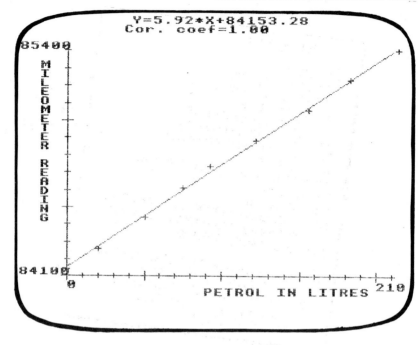

Screen Display 10.1

ii. If you run a car, try recording your mileage each time you fill up for petrol. Guess the petrol left in the tank at the time and record the petrol put in. You will now be able to keep an accurate track of how your car is performing. In recording this program, you automatically store your previous petrol consumption figures with it. So next time you fill up with petrol, you merely have to load in your existing program and add to the data. Any changes should be immediately obvious from the display.

iii. Modify the data for Listing 10.1 by neglecting the estimated petrol remaining in the tank, i.e. setting it to zero for all the data. How does this affect the equation of the straight line and the correlation coefficient?

```
Listing 10.1

10 READ N
20 DIM X(N+1),Y(N)
30 X(Ø)=N :X(1)=Ø
40 FOR I=1 TO N
50   READ Y(I),X(I+1),S
60   X(I+1)=X(I+1)+X(I)
70   IF I>1 THEN X(I)=X(I)-S
80   NEXT I
90 MODE4:VDU19,1,3;Ø;19,Ø,4;Ø;
100 PROCgraph
110 PROCbstln
120 PROCnamex("PETROL IN LITRES")
130 PROCnamey("MILEOMETER READING")
140 VDU5:MOVEØ,1050:END
150
160 DATA 9 ,84140,30,0 ,84260,20,10
    ,84442,25,0 ,84612,30,0
170 DATA 84733,20,13 ,84881,30,3
    ,85060,30,0 ,85231,30,3
180 DATA 85400,30,2
```

10.5 Setting the accuracy of the equation and the correlation coefficient

When PROCbstln evaluates the equation of the best straight line and the correlation coefficient, it prints them out, corrected to two decimal places. We chose this accuracy quite arbitrarily to prevent the equation looking too clumsy, but we have made provision for you to alter it if you want. PROCbstln includes the following statement at line 10870:

@%=&20204

It sets the number of decimal places to 2, but you can vary this up to an accuracy of 9 significant figures. The number of decimal places - currently 2 - is given by the third digit after the ampersand &. If you increase this, you will accordingly have to alter the space within which the number is printed. This space - at present set to 4 - is given by the last digit.

```
This program will draw the best

straight line through a number of

points which you provide as

co-ordinates. When you are asked for

the co-ordinates of each point, please

type the X co-ordinate first, then a

comma, then the Y co-ordinate. Then

press RETURN.


How many points do you want ?6
Co-ordinates of point 1?1.1,2
Co-ordinates of point 2?2.5,3.2
Co-ordinates of point 3?4.3,5.0
Co-ordinates of point 4?6.7,6.8
Co-ordinates of point 5?7.3,7.9
Co-ordinates of point 6?8.5,8
```

Screen Display 10.2 (first part)

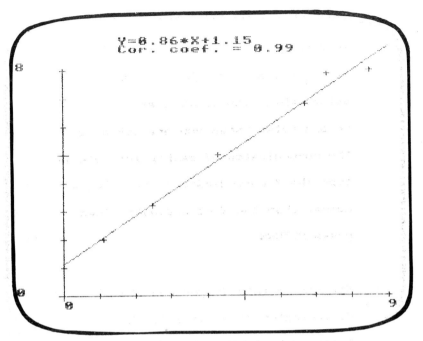

Screen Display 10.2 (second part)

10.6 Activities

___

Screen Display 10.2 shows the dialogue and screen display produced by running the program of Listing 10.2. The data that we, as users of the program have fed in, is underlined to distinguish it from that part of the dialogue which comes from the computer. This program is similar to that of Listing 10.1, except that it allows data to be entered at the time the program is run. Enter this program and run it. Then try going into PROCbstln to vary the accuracy with which the equation and correlation coefficient are printed out.

___

```
     Listing 10.2
10 MODE4:VDU19,1,3;0;19,0,4;0;
20 PRINT ' "This program will draw the best"
30 PRINT ' "straight line through a number of"
40 PRINT ' "points which you provide as"
50 PRINT ' "co-ordinates. When you are asked for"
60 PRINT ' "the co-ordinates of each point, please"
70 PRINT ' "type the X co-ordinate first, then a"
80 PRINT ' "comma, then the Y co-ordinate. Then"
90 PRINT ' "press RETURN."
100 INPUT ' ' ' "How many points do you want ",N
110 DIM X(N),Y(N)
120 FOR I=1 TO N
130    PRINT ' "Co-ordinates of point ";I;
140    INPUT X(I),Y(I)
150    NEXT I
160 X(0)=N
170
180 CLG
190 PROCgraph
200 PROCbstln
210 VDU5 :MOVE 0,1100 :END
```

11 Displaying shapes of functions

11.0 Introduction

In this chapter we provide and explain programs by which you can display the shapes of functions. There are many situations where it is useful to able to do this, perhaps to get some idea whether a function doubles back on itself, or whether it reaches a maximum or a minimum - and if so, where. In fact, a standard

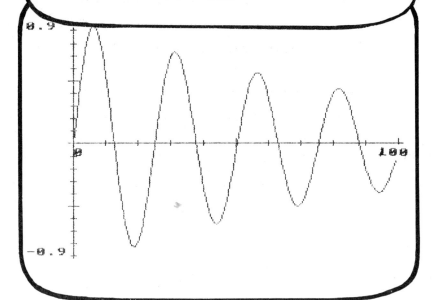

This program will draw the shape
produced by any function, provided
it is expressed in BASIC.

Please enter the function when you
see the prompt Y=

Press the space bar when you are
ready to begin.

Y=EXP(-X/100)*SIN(X/4)

What is the smallest value of X ?0

What is the largest value of X ?100

How many steps ?100

Screen Display 11.1

```
    Listing 11.1
10 MODE4 :VDU 19,0,4;0;19,1,3;0;
20 PRINT ' ' ' ' '
30 PRINT "This program will draw the shape"
40 PRINT "produced by any function, provided"
50 PRINT "it is expressed in BASIC." '
60 PRINT "Please enter the function when you"
70 PRINT "see the prompt Y="
80 PRINT ' ' "Press the space bar when you are"
90 PRINT "ready to begin." ' '
100 IF GET<>32 THEN 100
110 INPUT "Y=",A$
120 INPUT ' "What is the smallest value of X ",SX$
130 SX=EVAL(SX$)
140 INPUT ' "What is the largest value of X ",LX$
150 LX=EVAL(LX$)
160 INPUT ' "How many steps ",step%
170 PRINT
180 VDU3
190
200 DIM X(step%),Y(step%)
210
220 REM Work out largest and smallest Y
230 X=SX:Y(1)=EVAL(A$):Y(2)=Y(1)
240 FOR X=SX TO LX STEP (LX-SX)/step%
250    £Y=EVAL(A$)
260    IFY(2)<£Y THEN Y(2)=£Y
270    IFY(1)>£Y THEN Y(1)=£Y
280    NEXTX
290 X(0)=2 :X(1)=SX :X(2)=LX
300                     410    DRAW FN£CVX(X),FN£CVY(EVAL(A$))
310 CLG                 420    NEXTX
320 PROCscale           430
330 PROCaxes            440 VDU5 :MOVE 0,1100 :END
340 PROCgraduate
350 PROCnumber
360 PRINT TAB(10,1);"Y=";A$
370
380 REM Now display graph
390 X=X(1):MOVE FN£CVX(X),FN£CVY(EVAL(A$))
400 FOR X=X(1) TO X(2) STEP (X(2)-X(1))/step%
```

method for solving simultaneous equations relies on the technique of displaying the shapes of the functions concerned and identifying where they coincide.

Even if you do not want to use our programs for any specific purpose, you will find it fun just to experiment and see the shapes that various functions produce. In doing so, you will also be gaining some worthwhile mathematical insights.

11.1 Selecting a function for display

Our programs are suitable for displaying functions with two variables. We arbitrarily call these X and Y, although they could of course be called anything else. Such functions produce a display in two dimensions. Our programs are not suitable for displaying functions with more than two variables, because these would need at least three dimensions.

In order to use our programs to display functions, you have to feed in the function in the following form, where the dots represent an expression which the computer can evaluate:

$$Y = ...$$

The Y must be alone on the left-hand side. This means that expressions such as the following need some prior manipulation before they are suitable:

$$2Y + \sin X = 3$$
$$Y \sin X = 5$$
$$6 \cos X + Y \sin X + \tan X = 0$$

The expression for X can be as complex as you like, provided it is written in terms that the computer can recognise and use. The following are suitable examples:

```
Y=SIN(X/9)/SQR(X)
Y=SQR(X^2+45*X)
Y=EXP(-X/98.2)*SIN(X/41)
```

11.2 Using the function-drawing program

Before we discuss the program which draws the functions, you may like to see what it can do. We shall take the following function as an example, which - incidentally - is for damped oscillatory motion:

$$Y=EXP(-X/98.2)*SIN(X/41)$$

Screen Display 11.1 shows the requests that the program makes to the user: about the function required; about the smallest value of X and the largest value of X; and about the number of steps. (Our example data is underlined to distinguish it from the part of the dialogue which is due to the computer rather than to the user.) Screen Display 11.1 also shows the resulting display for the data which we provide. You could of course input other data and get a very different display.

11.3 The operation of the program

Listing 11.1 gives the program responsible for Screen Display 11.1. As you are probably coming to expect, it relies on PROCscale, PROCgraduate and PROCnumber. We do not use PROCgraph on this occasion because PROCgraph plots each point as a small + whereas we want a continuous curve. We use the DRAW statement of BBC BASIC. However, by calling upon PROCscale, we still take advantage of the automatic scaling which so simplifies the programming. To convert from the X and Y co-ordinates supplied by the program to the numbers required when addressing the screen, we have included two functions within PROCscale: FN'CVX and FN'CVY. At any place where your program wishes to write to the screen, the scaling is done automatically if, in place of X and Y, you use FN'CVX(X) and FN'CVY(Y). Therefore line 390 draws the continuous curve by repeated references to:

$$DRAW\ FN'CVX(X),FN'CVY(EVAL(A\$))$$

The program starts with some PRINT statements about what it can do. Once the function is entered, it is evaluated in response to the statement EVAL in line 210, 230, 370 and 390. In case this statement is unfamiliar to you, we now discuss it briefly. Essentially the program requests the user to type in a valid BASIC expression in a line such as:

110 INPUT"Y="A$

Suppose the user types in, say, 2*X+5 as response. The INPUT statement then gives A$ this value. Suppose also that the next line of the program uses A$ in an expression involving EVAL in the following form:

```
This program will simultaneously
display the shapes produced by two
functions, provided that they are
both expressed in BASIC.

Please enter each function as you
are requested.


Press the space bar when you are
ready to begin.

Now enter the first function:

Y=EXP(X/40)*COS(X/2)


Now enter the second function:

Y=2+COS(X/2)

What is the smallest value of X ?0

What is the largest value of X ?100

How many steps?100
```

Screen Display 11.2a (first part)

      120 Y=EVAL(A$)

The result is identical to what would have happened if lines 110 and 120 had been replaced by:

      110 Y=2*X+5

The use of EVAL, however, allows a different expression to be entered every time the program is run. If you enter a function that is impossible to evaluate, for example, one involving the square root of a negative number, you will get an error message.

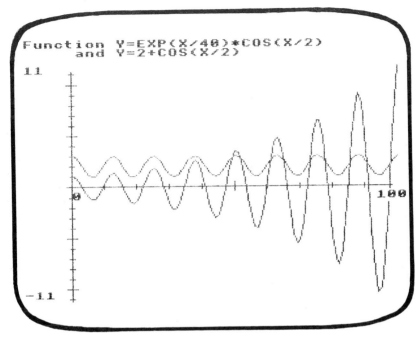

Screen Display 11.2a (second part)

     The program next asks for the range of values of X for which to display the equation. It then evaluates the smallest and largest values of X and Y in the display, by working through all the possible points that it will later plot. An error message can be produced at this stage. It might be because the equation produces too large a value for display or because of a division by zero. It is impossible to check for these in advance.

     The program may take some time to run, as it works out the co-ordinates for each point twice: once to find the smallest and largest and secondly to plot the points with an appropriate scaling. Consequently the program may pause during execution. The delay depends on the complexity of the calculation and the number of points required. This number can be as small as 20 for a near straight line relationship, but should be more like 100 for a more complex curve.

```
   Listing 11.2
 10 MODE4:VDU19,0,4;0;19,1,3;0;
 20 PRINT ' ' '
 30 PRINT "This program will simultaneously"
 40 PRINT "display the shapes produced by two"
 50 PRINT "functions, provided that they are"
 60 PRINT "both expressed in BASIC." '
 70 PRINT "Please enter each function as you"
 80 PRINT "are requested." '
 90 PRINT ' ' "Press the space bar when you are"
100 PRINT "ready to begin." ' '
110 IF GET<>32 THEN 110
120 PRINT "Now enter the first function:" '
130 INPUT "Y="A$
140 PRINT ' ' "Now enter the second function:" '
150 INPUT "Y="B$
160 INPUT ' "What is the smallest value of X ",SX$
170 SX=EVAL(SX$)
180 INPUT ' "What is the largest value of X ",LX$
190 LX=EVAL(LX$)
200 INPUT ' "How many steps",step :step=(LX-SX)/step
210
220 DIM X((LX-SX)/step),Y((LX-SX)/step)
230
240 REM Work out largest and smallest Y
250 X=SX:Y(1)=EVAL(A$):Y(2)=Y(1)
260 FOR X=SX TO LX STEP step
270    £Y=EVAL(A$)  :£Z=EVAL(B$)
280    IFY(2)<£Y THEN Y(2)=£Y
290    IFY(2)<£Z THEN Y(2)=£Z
300    IFY(1)>£Y THEN Y(1)=£Y
310    IFY(1)>£Z THEN Y(1)=£Z
320    NEXTX
330 X(0)=2 :X(1)=SX :X(2)=LX
340
350 MODE4:VDU19,0,4;0;19,1,3;0;
360 PROCscale
370 PROCaxes
380 PROCgraduate
390 PROCnumber
400 PRINT TAB(10,1);"Y=";A$
410 PRINT TAB(6,2);"and Y=";B$                    P.T.O.
```

```
Listing 11.2  continued
420 REM Now display graph
430 X=X(1):MOVE FN£CVX(X),FN£CVY(EVAL(A$))
440 FOR X=X(1) TO X(2) STEP step
450    DRAW FN£CVX(X),FN£CVY(EVAL(A$))
460    NEXTX
470
480 REM Now display second graph
490 X=X(1):MOVE FN£CVX(X),FN£CVY(EVAL(B$))
500 FOR X=X(1) TO X(2) STEP step
510    DRAW FN£CVX(X),FN£CVY(EVAL(B$))
520    NEXTX
530
540 VDU5:MOVE0,1050:END
```

11.4 Activities

i. Run the program of Listing 11.1 with various functions of your own choosing.

ii. Experiment to see the effect of varying the smallest and largest values of X and the number of steps.

iii. Purposely choose an expression which will result in a division by zero to see the error message produced.

11.5 Displaying two functions together

It is often interesting to display two functions together. For example, you can see where they coincide and hence solve them as simultaneous equations. For viewing two functions on the screen simultaneously, the automatic scaling has to take into account the smallest and largest values of both functions over the range of plotting. This means that you may have to put in some thought when entering the functions. Otherwise the automatic

```
This program will simultaneously
display the shapes produced by two
functions, provided that they are
both expressed in BASIC.

Please enter each function as you
are requested.


Press the space bar when you are
ready to begin.


Now enter the first function:

Y=EXP(X/40)*COS(X/2)


Now enter the second function:

Y=2+COS(X/2)

What is the smallest value of X ?48

What is the largest value of X ?53

How many steps?100
```

Screen Display 11.2b (first part)

scaling may make one negligibly small compared with the other,
as it has to ensure that the composite fills the screen.

In order to display two functions, the program of Listing 11.1
is extended and is given as Listing 11.2. Screen Display 11.2a
shows the result for plotting the following two functions:

$$Y=EXP(X/40)*COS(X/2)$$

and

$$Y=2+COS(X/2)$$

You can more precisely identify the point where the two graphs

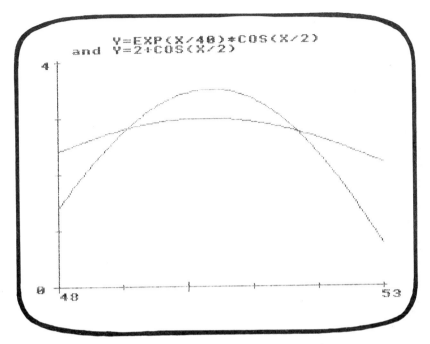

Screen Display 11.2b (second part)

intersect by reducing the range of values of X for the screen display. We illustrate with Screen Display 11.2b. The functions are the same, but, as you will see from the dialogue between the program and the person running it, the plot is over a smaller range of values for X.

11.6 Activities

i. Use the method of plotting two functions together to solve the following simultaneous equations.

$$Y = SIN(X)$$
$$Y = TAN(X)$$

Do you get an error message? If so, why might this be? (See Section 1.7.)

ii. Experiment with the range of X values and see how precisely you can get the solution.

iii. Choose some more pairs of functions and solve them as simultaneous equations.

11.7 Discussion of activities

Activity 11.6 i: You might get an error message because TAN(X) goes to infinity if the range of values is not wisely chosen.

12 Drawing histograms

12.0 Introduction

Histograms provide a simple and dramatic way of displaying the relative frequencies with which events or items occur. In this chapter we show how to draw various types of histograms to display data. The programs rely on one of two procedures: PROChisto and PROC3Dhisto, which are two more of the procedures which we provide for you. PROChisto which draws up bars with suitable height and spacing for the data you supply and PROC3Dhisto which does the same, except that the bars are drawn with a mock perspective to give a three dimensional 'tower' effect. You must use the procedures with PROCscale so that your display automatically fits nicely onto the screen, and you can also optionally call on PROCnamex, PROCnamey, PROCgraduate and PROClabel. Like all our other procedures, PROChisto and PROC3Dhisto are listed in Appendix 1 and are also available, ready-recorded, on cassette tape.

12.1 Drawing a simple histogram

A histogram shows the relative frequencies with which various events or items occur. Examples could be the numbers of cars, lorries, bicycles and pedestrians passing a road junction between certain hours; or the numbers of calories in different types of food. As an illustration, Screen Display 12.1 shows such a histogram for the cost of a holiday in an English resort, according to times of year. The histogram makes it is obvious at a glance that summer is the most expensive time, and that winter is the cheapest.

Listing 12.1 gives the program which produces Screen Display 12.1. It breaks naturally into three parts, namely: the input section to tell the computer how many bars are to be drawn and the frequencies that they are to represent; the scaling and axes-drawing section; and the histogram-drawing section, which uses the data and appropriate scaling to produce the display. The data could have been inputted in several ways. We chose to use the INPUT statement because it is a convenient and quick way of getting data into the program and allows a rapid presentation of any data in histogram form. (For displays which are to be recorded for later display, DATA statements are preferable, as illustrated in our later examples.) The sections which call on PROCscale, draw the axes and draw the histogram are self-evident, because they rely on the procedures which we provide.

12.2 Activities

Run the program of Listing 12.1 and input some data of your choice.

This program will draw a histogram
from data which you supply. When
requested, please enter how many bars
you require and the frequency or
quantity that each bar should represent.

Press the space bar when you are
ready to begin.

How many bars do you require?12
What frequency for bar 1 ?113
What frequency for bar 2 ?113
What frequency for bar 3 ?113
What frequency for bar 4 ?123
What frequency for bar 5 ?126
What frequency for bar 6 ?142
What frequency for bar 7 ?157
What frequency for bar 8 ?157
What frequency for bar 9 ?148
What frequency for bar 10 ?126
What frequency for bar 11 ?126
What frequency for bar 12 ?126

Screen Display 12.1 (first part)

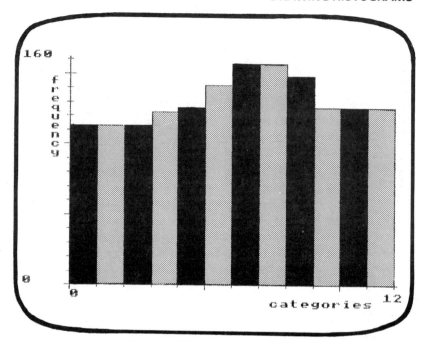

Screen Display 12.1 (second part)

12.3 Labelling the bars

It is possible to label the bars of a histogram, but it is rather
time-consuming because it involves a certain amount of trial,
error and experiment. You will almost certainly only want to
bother for a permanent display, in which case you will want to
put in the data using DATA statements. Listing 12.2 and Screen
Display 12.2 illustrate such a histogram. Several options are
available for labelling the bars. For example, you can use the
TAB function, as explained in Section 9.5; or you can issue the
command VDU5 which makes all the printing which follows at a
position dictated by the current graphics cursor. To print starting
at the centre of the screen use:

```
VDU5
MOVE 640,512
PRINT "message"
```

```
    Listing 12.1
10 MODE1 :VDU19,0,4;0;19,3,3;0;
20 PRINT ' "This program will draw a histogram"
30 PRINT ' "from data which you supply. When"
40 PRINT ' "requested, please enter how many bars"
50 PRINT ' "you require and the frequency or"
60 PRINT ' "quantity that each bar should represent."
70 PRINT ' ' "Press the space bar when you are"
80 PRINT ' "ready to begin."
90 G=GET :IF G<>32 THEN 90
100 INPUT ' ' "How many bars do you require",B
110 DIM X(B+1),Y(B+1)
120
130 FOR I%=1 TO B
140    PRINT ' "What frequency for bar ";I%;" ";
150    INPUT Y(I%) :X(I%)=I%
160    NEXT I%
170
180 X(0)=B+1:Y(B+1)=0 :£IN=1
190
200 CLG
210 VDU19,0,4;0; :REM change colours for bars
220 VDU19,2,1;0;
230 VDU19,3,7;0;
240 VDU19,1,2;0;
250
260 PROCscale
270 PROChisto
280 GCOL0,3
290 PROCaxes
300 PROCgraduate
310 PROCnumber
320 PROCnamex("categories")
330 PROCnamey("frequency")
340
350 VDU5:MOVE2000,2000:END
```

In Listing 12.2 we use the VDU5 statement as it is perhaps the simplest for you to modify for your own purpose.

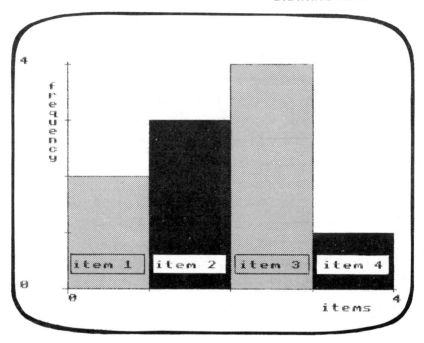

Screen Display 12.2

12.4 Activities

Run Listing 12.2 with some items of your own and experiment to
get the best positioning for the labels of the categories.

12.5 Drawing solid-looking histograms

Histograms can look particularly impressive if the bars are
separated and appear to have depth. Such a histogram is
demonstrated in Screen Display 12.3 which shows the numbers of
students passing a certain exam during the years from 1970 to
1983. The dip around 1976 represents a fall in popularity of the
subject. Listing 12.3 gives the program for the Screen Display.

```
     Listing 12.2
10 DATA 4
20 DATA 2,3,4,1
30 RESTORE :READ B
40 DIM X(B+1),Y(B+1)
50
60 X(0)=B+1:Y(B+1)=0 :£IN=1
70 MODE 1
80
90 FOR I=1 TO X(0)-1
100    READ Y(I) :X(I)=I*£IN
110    NEXT I
120
130
140 VDU19,0,4;0; :REM change
       colours for bars
150 VDU19,2,1;0;
160 VDU19,3,7;0;
170 VDU19,1,2;0;
180
190 PROCscale
200 PROChisto
210 GCOL0,3
220 PROCaxes
230 PROCgraduate
240 PROCnumber
250 PROCnamex("items")
260 PROCnamey("frequency")
270 VDU5:MOVE160,200:PRINT"item 1
       item 2   item 3   item 4"
280
290 VDU5:MOVE2000,2000:END
```

12.6 Activities

Run the program of Listing 12.3, using your own data.

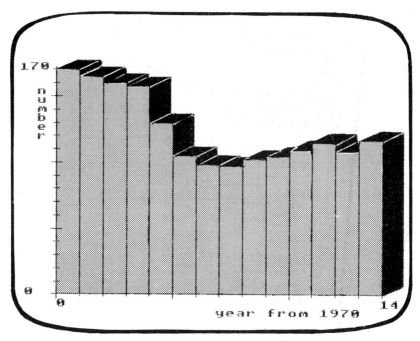

Screen Display 12.3

12.7 Drawing two histograms together

You can display the histograms for two sets of data together, so making it easier to compare and contrast them. The technique lends itself particularly to the separate-column, solid-looking type of display, of the previous section. Screen Display 12.4 illustrates the effect. The front bars show the frequency with which various heights occurred amongst female students and the back bars show the corresponding frequencies for the male students. The contrast is obvious at a glance and easily compensates for the greater difficulty in reading the heights from the scales.

The program, which is given in Listing 12.4, requires only slight modification from that of Listing 12.3. It uses a FOR...NEXT loop between lines 110 and 250. The origin of the

```
        Listing 12.3
10 DATA 14
20 DATA 170,165,160,158,130,105,98
30 DATA 97,102,105,110,115,108,117
40 RESTORE :READ B
50 DIM X(B+1),Y(B+1)
60
70 X(Ø)=B+1:Y(B+1)=Ø :£IN=1
80 MODE 1
90
100 FOR I=1 TO X(Ø)-1
110    READ Y(I) :X(I)=I*£IN
120    NEXT I
130
140
150 VDU19,Ø,4;Ø; :REM change colours
       for bars
160 VDU19,2,1;Ø;
170 VDU19,3,7;Ø;
180 VDU19,1,2;Ø;
190
200 PROCscale
210 PROC3Dhisto(1)
220 GCOLØ,3
230 PROCaxes
240 PROCgraduate
250 PROCnumber
260 PROCnamex("year from 1970")
270 PROCnamey("number")
280
290 VDU5:MOVE2000,2000:END
```

graphics co-ordinates is reset between the two loops, using a VDU29,X;Y; command in line 160. This forces the origin for the rest of the graphics to be displaced to the point X,Y, so placing one set of bars slightly above and to the right of the other. This makes the second set of bars appear behind the first. As the second set of bars are drawn after and in front of the first, they hide the parts of the first which should be out of sight.

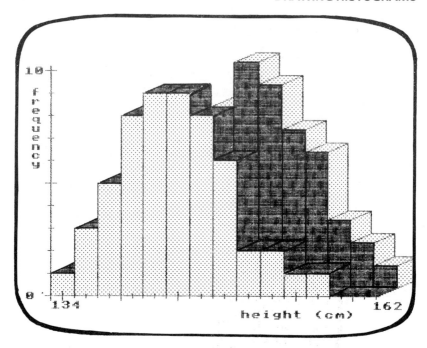

Screen Display 12.4

12.8 Activities

i. Run the program of Listing 12.4 with your own data.

ii. Try altering the VDU29,X;Y; statement to shift the
displacement of one set of bars behind the other.

```
    Listing 12.4
10 DATA 14
20 DATA 1,1,2,3,4,7,8,10,9,7,6,3,2,1
30 DATA 1,3,5,8,9,9,8,6,2,2,1,1,0,0
40 RESTORE :READ B
50 DIM X(B+1),Y(B+1)
60
70 X(0)=B+1:Y(B+1)=0 :£IN=2
80 X(B+1)=134
90 MODE 1
100
110 FOR G=1 TO 0 STEP -1
120   FOR I=1 TO X(0)-1
130     READ Y(I) :X(I)=I*£IN+134
140     NEXT I
150
160   VDU 29,G*64;G*32;
170
180   VDU19,0,4;0; :REM change colours
      for bars
190   VDU19,2,1;0;
200   VDU19,3,7;0;
210   VDU19,1,2;0;
220
230   IF G=1 THEN PROCscale
240   PROC3Dhisto(2-G)
250   NEXT G
260 GCOL0,3
270 PROCaxes
280 PROCgraduate
290 PROCnumber
300 PROCnamey("frequency")
310 PROCnamex("height (cm)")
320
330 VDU5:MOVE2000,2000:END
```

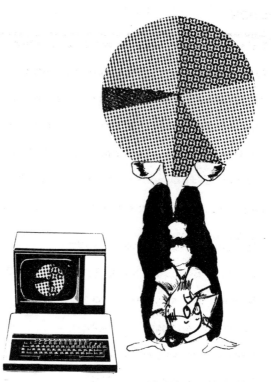

13 Drawing pie charts

13.0 Introduction

A pie chart is a display which shows the relative amounts of things which make up a whole. The whole is represented by a complete circle, and each of the other quantities is represented by a segment of the circle. With a pie chart, it is easy to see proportions at a glance - something which is not so easy from a table of numbers.

154

This program will draw a pie chart
from data which you supply. When
requested, please enter the radius of
the pie chart, the co-ordinates of the
centre of the pie chart (as X,Y), the
number of segments, the value that each
segment is to represent and how each is
is to be labelled.
 Radius of pie chart ?<u>300</u>

 Centre of pie chart X,Y ?<u>700,512</u>

 Number of segments ?<u>6</u>

 Size of segment 1 ?<u>399</u>

 Label for segment 1?<u>Model B</u>

 Size of segment 2 ?<u>105</u>

 Label for segment 2?<u>Disk interface</u>

 Size of segment 3 ?<u>295</u>

 Label for segment 3?<u>Disk drives</u>

 Size of segment 4 ?<u>280</u>

 Label for segment 4?<u>Monitor</u>

 Size of segment 5 ?<u>350</u>

 Label for segment 5?<u>Printer</u>

 Size of segment 6 ?<u>71</u>

 Label for segment 6?<u>Misc.</u>

Screen Display 13.1 (first part)

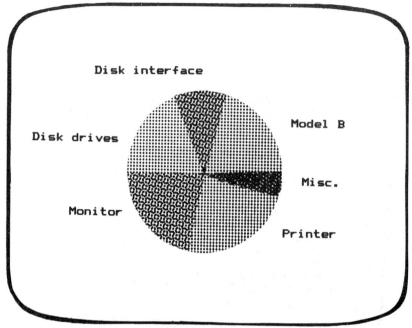

Screen Display 13.1 (second part)

This chapter shows how to draw pie charts. The programs rely on PROCpie which is one of the procedures which we provide. It draws a pie chart from data which you supply and of a size and positioning which you dictate. Like our other procedures PROCpie is given in Appendix 1 and is also available ready-recorded on cassette tape.

13.1 Drawing a pie chart

Screen Display 13.1 shows a pie chart for how a person might chose to divide up £1500 when buying a computer system. As a list, the figures are:

Model B BBC Computer	£399
Disk interface	£105
Disk drives	£295
Colour monitor	£280
Printer	£350
Miscellaneous	£71
TOTAL	£1500

```
      Listing 13.1
  10 MODE7
  20 PRINT ' "This program will draw a pie chart"
  30 PRINT ' "from data which you supply. When"
  40 PRINT ' "requested, please enter the radius of"
  50 PRINT ' "the pie chart, the co-ordinates of the"
  60 PRINT ' "centre of the pie chart (as X,Y), the"
  70 PRINT ' "number of segments, the value that each"
  80 PRINT ' "segment is to represent and how each is"
  90 PRINT ' "is to be labelled."
 100 INPUT ' ' "Radius of pie chart ",RA
 110 INPUT ' "Centre of pie chart X,Y ",XP,YP
 120 INPUT ' "Number of segments ",£NS
 130 DIM £S(£NS),£N$(£NS)
 140 £TO=0
 150 FOR I=1 TO £NS
 160    PRINT ' "Size of segment ";I;" ";
 170    INPUT £S(I)
 180    £TO=£TO+£S(I)
 190    PRINT ' "Label for segment ";I;
 200    INPUT £N$(I)
 210    NEXT I
 220 MODE 1 :VDU19,0,4;0; :REM MODE 5 for Model A
 230 PROCpie(RA,XP,YP,£TO)
 240 PROClabel(RA,XP,YP,£TO)
 250 VDU5 :MOVE 2000,2000 :END
```

Compared with this list, you will probably agree that the division of resources is more obvious at a glance from Screen Display 13.1.

Listing 13.1 gives the program for producing Screen Display 13.1. Lines 100 and 110 ask the user for the radius and centre of the required pie chart. This data is fed in via INPUT statements which provide for a dialogue between the computer and a user. (Our data is underlined to distinguish it from the computer's part of the dialogue. You could of course input yours instead of ours.) When you come to do so, we suggest that you identify the centre of the pie chart with addressable points around 600, 500, and that you choose a radius of something less than 400. All of these measurements are in screen co-ordinates, as measured in addressable points (see Section 1.4). The rest of the program relies on PROCpie which takes care of drawing the display.

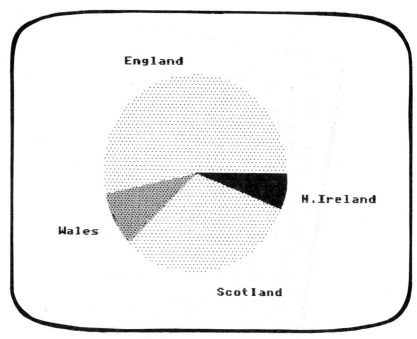

Screen Display 13.2

13.2 Activities

i. Run the program of Listing 13.1 using your own data.

ii. Draw several pie charts, each one at a different position on the screen and with a different radius.

iii. Can you accommodate a long sector name by specifying a new centre to move the pie chart sideways?

13.3 Storing a pie chart

When the data is fed in as INPUT statements, the resulting pie chart cannot easily be stored. You may therefore prefer to use DATA statements instead. Not only do they allow for easy

```
Listing 13.2
10 DATA 350,560,512
20 DATA 4
30 DATA 131,"England"
40 DATA 21,"Wales"
50 DATA 79,"Scotland"
60 DATA 14,"N.Ireland"
80 READ RA
90 READ XP,YP
100 READ £NS
110 DIM £S(£NS),£N$(£NS)
120 £TO=0
130 FOR I=1 TO £NS
140     READ £S(I)
150     £TO=£TO+£S(I)
160     READ £N$(I)
170     NEXT I
180 MODE 1 :VDU19,0,4;0; :REM
     MODE 5 for Model A
190 PROCpie(RA,XP,YP,£TO) :END
200 VDU5 :MOVE 2000,2000
```

storage, they are also easy to edit. Furthermore this means of programming makes it easier for you to add your own extras to the display. You could, for example, put in a title.

Screen Display 13.2 shows the relative areas of parts of the United Kingdom using the following data:

England	131000	square kilometres
Wales	21000	square kilometres
Scotland	79000	square kilometres
N.Ireland	14000	square kilometres

The data is stored in DATA statements and the complete program is given in Listing 13.2. This program works in the same way as that for Listing 13.1, apart from how the data is fed in. With this sort of program, you can load it, and keep editing and experimenting until you are completely satisfied with the display.

13.4 Activities

---

i. Run the program of Listing 13.2 using some data of your own.

ii. Experiment with the positioning and labelling until you are satisfied with the result.

14 Displaying statistics

14.0 Introduction

Statistics is the mathematical treatment of sets of data. In this chapter we deal with the simple statistics of a set of measurements which might be expected to be randomly distributed around a steady or mean value. The measurements could be the weights or heights of a group of people; or the exam marks of a class.

The program in this chapter displays such sets of data. It also calculates and displays the mean of the measurements, their standard deviation and the standard error on the mean. Then it superimposes the shape of a normal (or Gaussian) distribution with the same standard error, so that you can decide whether your data follows the standard distribution closely enough for your purpose.

14.1 Some statistical terms

Our statistics program calculates and prints the mean of a set of measurements, their standard deviation and the standard error on the mean. The meanings of these terms are as follows:

The mean $\bar{x}$ of a set of n measurements is given by the following formula where Σ means 'sum of':

$$\bar{x} = \frac{\Sigma x}{n}$$

The standard deviation σ is given by the following formula:

$$\sigma = \sqrt{\frac{\Sigma(x - \bar{x})^2}{n - 1}}$$

The standard error on the mean $\sigma_{\bar{x}}$ is given by:

$$\sigma_{\bar{x}} = \frac{\sigma}{\sqrt{n}}$$

The normal or Gaussian distribution has the following formula:

$$y = \frac{1}{\sigma\sqrt{(2\pi)}} \exp \frac{-(x - \bar{x})^2}{2\sigma^2}$$

It can be recognised by its characteristic bell-shaped curve which is symmetrical about the mean.

14.2 The statistics program

The statistics program is given in Listing 14.1. Screen Display 14.1 is typical of what it can do. The measurements are for the percentage alcohol in home made wines. They were collected over a number of years from members of an evening class on wine making, and total 56 measurements. All the members were making the same wine to the same recipe, so variations could be expected to be randomly distributed about a mean or a fixed value.

As Screen Display 14.1 shows, the distribution does not follow the normal (or Gaussian) distribution because it is not bell-shaped and symmetrical about the mean. Possibly some of the wines did not ferment to completion whereas the majority did. The majority should therefore be close to the maximum possible value while the others tail down to zero. The mean of the measurements, the standard deviation and the standard error on the mean are all printed on the screen.

The listing is a little longer than those that you will have come to expect. This is because the lines which work out the mean, the standard deviation and the standard error on the mean are in the program, rather than in a separate procedure.

The program stores the information in the form of DATA statements. This is important, for in such a program there may be very many items. These must be in a form which can easily be checked and edited. For Screen Display 14.1, there are 56 items in the DATA statements, and such a large number is bound to need careful checking for accurate transcription.

The program lines between 110 and 160 calculate the sum of the data in preparation for lines 210 to 260 which calculate the mean and the standard deviation and line 690 which calculates the standard error on the mean from the formulae given in Section 14.1. Line 290 then dimensions the X and Y arrays while 310 calls on PROCscale. When doing so, it uses just two points corresponding to the maximum and minimum data items. This sets up the scaling and allows lines 320 and 330 to arrange that the bars of the histogram fit in neatly with the graduations along the axes. These lines arrange that there will be at least 5 bars and not more than 15. If you do not like these limits, you can alter them accordingly.

Lines 350 to 380 assign the X co-ordinates for the histogram bars. With the number of bars set up and the co-ordinates of the bars calculated, the next task is to find the frequencies with which the data items fit the bar categories. This is what lines 410 to 460 do.

One further call to PROCscale at line 500 allows the scaling to be set up in the Y direction, that in the X direction remaining unchanged. A call to PROChisto draws up the bars and PROCaxes, PROCgraduate and PROCnumber put in the axes and scales.

Finally the normal distribution is drawn using the XOR method of plotting, set up by GCOL3,1 in line 560. Lines 580 to 600 then calculate 100 points along the normal distribution function and plot them using the DRAW statement.

14.3 Activities

---

i. Run the program of Listing 14.1 using your own data.

ii. Save the program, retrieve it and edit it in some way.

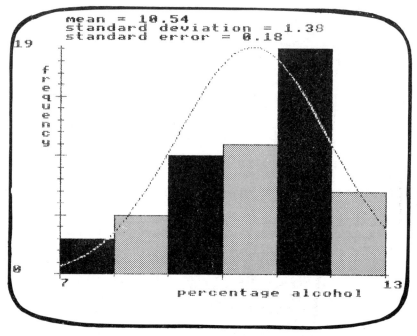

Screen Display 14.1

14.4 Superimposing alternative distributions

You may like to compare your distribution with some distribution other than the normal, Gaussian distribution - perhaps with the Poisson distribution or the Binomial distribution. You can easily do so by modifying lines 570 and 590 of Listing 14.1 which calculate and display the shape of the normal, Gaussian distribution with the same standard error. The formula for the Gaussian distribution is given in Section 14.1. In BASIC the right-hand side becomes:

K*EXP(-(X-MEN)*(X-MEN)/(2*SI*SI))/SI

This is used in lines 570 and 590, and you can easily replace it with an expression for another distribution.

```
   Listing 14.1
10 REM Read in data
20 DATA 56
30 DATA 12,12.2,11,11.3,13,11.2,9.8,8.3,11.6,12.3,8.2
40 DATA 11.3,11.7,10.5,10.3,11.8,9.8,12,11.1,10.1,12
50 DATA 8.5,8.9,9.3,9.9,11,9.2,10.5,11.3,9.8,10.8,11
60 DATA 11.9,7.8,12.5,10.5,10.3,9.4,11.6,11.3,11.2,12.1
70 DATA 8.9,9.5,10.2,10.6,10.9,9.0,11.5,11.6,11.9
80 DATA 7,7,9.5,10.5,11.9
90 READ NUM
100 READ SM :LAR=SM :tot=SM
110 FOR I=2 TO NUM
120    READ V
130    IF V<SM THEN SM=V
140    IF V>LAR THEN LAR=V
150    tot=tot+V
160    NEXT I
170
180 REM Calculate the MEan and SIgma
190
200 RESTORE 30
210 MEN=tot/NUM :SI=0
220 FOR I=1 TO NUM
230    READ V
240    SI=SI+(V-MEN)^2
250    NEXT I
260 SI=SQR(SI/(NUM-1))
270
280 REM scaling for x range
290 DIM X(17),Y(17)
300 X(0)=2 :X(1)=SM :X(2)=LAR :Y(1)=SM :Y(2)=LAR
310 PROCscale
320 D=£LH-£LL :IF D<5 THEN D=D*2
330 IF D>15 THEN D=INT(D/2)
340
350 FOR I=1 TO D
360    X(I)=£SX+(£LX-£SX)*I/D
370    Y(I)=0
380    NEXT I                          P.T.O.
390
```

```
      Listing 14.1     continued
400 MAXY=0 :RESTORE 30
410 FOR I=1 TO NUM
420   READ V
430   X=(V-£SX)*D/(£LX-£SX)+1
440   Y(X)=Y(X)+1
450   IF Y(X)>MAXY THEN MAXY=Y(X)
460   NEXT I
470
480 X(0)=D+1 :X(D+1)=£SX
490 REM rescale for y
500 PROCscale
510
520 MODE4:VDU19,0,4;0;19,1,3;0;
530 X(0)=D+1
540 £IN=(£LX-£SX)/D
550 PROChisto
560 GCOL3,1
570 MOVE FN£CVX(£SX),FN£CVY(7*EXP(-(£SX-MEN)*
      (£SX-MEN)/(2*SI*SI))/SI)
580 FOR X=£SX TO £LX STEP (£LX-£SX)/100
590   DRAW FN£CVX(X),FN£CVY(1.4*MAXY*EXP(-(X-MEN)*
      (X-MEN)/(2*SI*SI))/SI)
600   NEXT X
610 GCOL0,3
620 PROCaxes
630 PROCgraduate
640 PROCnumber
650 PROCnamex("percentage alcohol")
660 PROCnamey("frequency")
670 @%=&20204 :PRINT TAB(5,0);"mean = ";MEN
680 PRINT TAB(5,1);"standard deviation = ";SI
690 PRINT TAB(5,2);"standard error = ";SI/SQR(NUM)
700
710 VDU5:MOVE2000,2000:END
720 END
```

15 Using Teletext graphics

15.0 Introduction

Normally in mode 7, the mode in which the computer first turns on, you can only display black and white text. This chapter explains how to get the full range of eight ordinary colours and eight flashing colours for text and graphics using Teletext facilities. These facilities are only available in mode 7 and are as used by television's Ceefax and Oracle. The method by which the colours are written to the screen is completely different from the other modes, and the amount of memory taken up by the screen display is only 1K. This contrasts with the 10K taken up by modes 4 or 5 and means that more memory is available for sophisticated programs - which is especially important with a Model A BBC Microcomputer.

The appearance of Teletext graphics is somewhat coarser than in other modes, as there are only 78 pixels addressable across the screen and 75 vertically. For some displays this can be a disadvantage, but for others you can exploit it for dramatic effects, especially as the full range of colours is available.

Teletext facilities have to be turned on a line at a time. As this makes text as well as graphics programming very different from that in other modes, we shall deal with both in this chapter.

15.1 Writing in colour

Mode 7 provides a Teletext screen display of 25 lines with 40 characters to a line. To get colour on any one line, you need to print a character, called a control character, on that line. Each control character occupies one character position on the line but appears blank, ie as the screen's background colour. All the text to the right of the control character is affected by the control character; all the text to the left of the control character is not. The control character affects only the one line on which it is placed.

A control character can be inserted into a line using the PRINT statement. Table 15.1 gives the possible colour control codes for text. For example, suppose you want a display on the screen consisting of the single line:

     White Green Blue

Suppose that you also want each word to be in the same colour as its name. The following program achieves this using the appropriate colour control codes from Table 15.1:

```
10 MODE 7
20 PRINT "White";CHR$(130);"Green";CHR$(132);"Blue"
30 END
```

The colour code for white, ie 135, is the default control code. So you do not have to give a control code before "White" in the above line 20.

129	red text
130	green text
131	yellow text
132	blue text
133	magenta text
134	cyan text
135	white text

Table 15.1 Colour control codes for Teletext text

15.2 Colouring the background of a single line of text

You can set the background colour for each individual line of text. The instruction is the same as for text, except that you need two control characters, the first to control the colour and the second to specify that it is for the background. The following control characters change the colour of the background.

156 changes the background to black
157 changes the background colour to that for
    the preceding colour control code

For example, the following instruction sets a green background:

PRINT CHR$(130);CHR$(157)

15.3 Flashing text

You can get a very dramatic effect by making some of your text characters flash. You need the control code 136 which causes everything following it to flash between the foreground and background colours. You can turn off the flashing with code 137. For example, when the following line is executed, the word 'Flashing' flashes between red and black, while the word 'Steady' is printed in red and does not flash:

```
100 PRINT CHR$(136);CHR$(129);"Flashing"; CHR$(137);
    "Steady"
```

15.4 Making double height characters

You can also get dramatic effects by doubling the height of
Teletext text. This feature is achieved using two screen lines for
every line of text: one for the top half of the text and the other
for the bottom half. The doubling is turned on by code 141 and
off by code 140. For example the following two lines of program
print the message Double Height in characters twice the height
of normal characters.

```
100 PRINT CHR$(141);"Double Height"
110 PRINT CHR$(141);"Double Height"
```

The following two lines of program produce the message Double
Height in large letters next to the message Normal Height in
normal sized letters:

```
100 PRINT CHR$(141);"Double Height";CHR$(140);"Normal
    Height"
110 PRINT CHR$(141);"Double Height"
```

15.5 Activities

---

i. Enter the following and observe what happens:

```
10 MODE7
20 PRINTTAB(0,4);CHR$131;CHR$141;STRING$(5,"  Hello")
30 FORI=0TO33
40    PRINTTAB(I,5);CHR$131;CHR$141;"Hello"
50    FORT=1TO400:NEXTT
60    NEXTI
```

ii. Can you explain why the double height HELLO only appears
correctly on the screen some of the time? (See Section 15.13.)

145	red graphics
146	green graphics
147	yellow graphics
148	blue graphics
149	magenta graphics
150	cyan graphics
151	white graphics

Table 15.2 Colour control codes for Teletext graphics

15.6 Block graphics

You can get block graphics in a similar way to getting coloured text. You need the codes given in Table 15.2. The blocks of graphics all occupy one of the areas on the screen originally reserved for a letter, but any line starting with a code between 145 and 151 will no longer display lower case letters. In their place graphics characters appear. Although these codes cause lower case (small) letters, numbers and punctuation marks to appear as block graphics characters, upper case (capital) letters are unaffected. For example, in the first of the following two program lines, the code 131 causes yellow numbers to be printed. In the second line of program, the code 147 causes the printing to come out as yellow block graphics.

```
100 PRINT CHR$(131);"1234567890"
110 PRINT CHR$(147);"1234567890"
```

Each graphics character is made up of small blobs, 3 vertically and 2 horizontally. Thus a wide variety of block graphics characters are available, depending on which of the blobs are lit up. Table 15.3 gives the different types of block graphics which are available and their corresponding codes.

While using block graphics, you can get an attractive effect with control code 154, in conjunction with CHR$(147). This causes each block of graphics to be reduced in size, for example making a continuous line appear as a series of disconnected dots. Code 153 turns off the effect. This is particularly suitable for displaying curves and lines, as they appear less clumsy and of better resolution with the smaller sized blocks.

Double height block graphics can be obtained in the same way as with text, using the code 141.

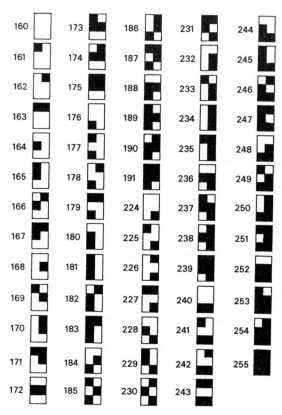

Table 15.3   Teletext block graphics

15.7 Getting continuity when changing colour

If, on one line, while printing a series of the same characters you change the colour, or height or some other characteristic, you normally get a space where the control character goes. This can spoil a graphics display. The problem may be solved by placing control code 158 to the left of the characters. Spaces for control codes will now be occupied with the previous character. This technique allows continous graphics displays, even where the colours change. Code 159 turns the effect off. For example, the following line causes a display of three red blocks, followed directly by 1 green block. No blank spaces can be seen, even though there is a change of colour caused by the code 146.

> 100 PRINT CHR$(145);CHR$(255);CHR$(158);CHR$(146); CHR$(255)

This is in contrast with the effect produced by the following lines which display a single red block followed by a space, where code 146 is stored, followed by a green block:

> 110 PRINT CHR$(145);CHR$(255);CHR$(146);CHR$(255)

Lines 100 and 110 may be put together to show both continuous and normal graphics on consecutive lines.

15.8 Composite figures

There are no user-definable characters in the Teletext mode. These are confined to the other graphics modes. However you can build up very satisfactory shapes by combining the block graphics shown in Table 15.4. You can place several characters together on a line merely by printing them together. For example, the following line of program produces the printout shown in Figure 15.1:

> 50 PRINT CHR$(149);"xyz"

You can make a composite figure on more than one line using the principles described for composite characters in other

Figure 15.1. The result of PRINT CHR$(149)"xyz".

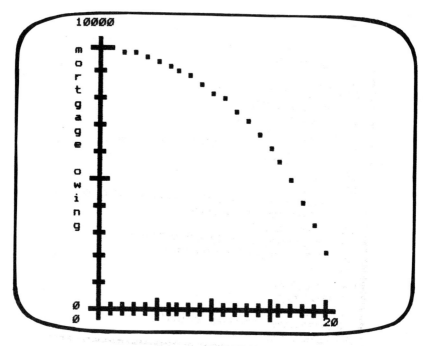

Screen Display 15.1

modes. These are in Section 4.6. Table 4.1 gives the appropriate codes. For your convenience, it is duplicated here as Table 15.4.

When writing a number of control codes, it is normally easier to use the VDU method whereby any VDU may be followed by as

ASCII code	result
08	move backwards one space
09	move forward one space
10	move down one line
11	move up one line

Table 15.4 Cursor control codes

```
    Listing 15.1

10 MODE7
20 PROCclg(4,3)
30 mortgage=10000
40 interestrate=13.5
50 monthpayments=120
60 DIM X(20),Y(20)   :REM X()=year count,
   Y()=mortgage
70 year=0
80 REPEAT
90    mortgage=mortgage+interestrate*mortgage/
      100-12*monthpayments
100   year=year+1
110   X(year)=year :Y(year)=mortgage
120   UNTIL year>19 OR mortgage<0
130
140 X(0)=year
150 PROCgraph
160 PROCnamex("year")
170 PROCnamey("mortgage owing")
180 REPEAT UNTIL 1=2
```

many codes as required. These codes may include character codes. For normal letters and numbers, the codes are the ASCII codes (see Appendix 3)

Figure 15.2 illustrates the sort of composite figure that can be constructed using Teletext graphics.

Figure 15.2. A composite figure consisting of Teletext block graphics.

This program will display the points
you provide as co-ordinates, a
pair at a time. When you are asked for
the co-ordinates of each point, please
type the X co-ordinate first, then a
comma, then the Y co-ordinate. Then
press RETURN.

How many points do you want ?10
Co-ordinates of point 1?1974,100
Co-ordinates of point 2?1975,100
Co-ordinates of point 3?1976,101
Co-ordinates of point 4?1977,101
Co-ordinates of point 5?1978,102
Co-ordinates of point 6?1979,102
Co-ordinates of point 7?1980,103
Co-ordinates of point 8?1981,104
Co-ordinates of point 9?1982,106
Co-ordinates of point 10?1983,110

Screen Display 15.2 (first part)

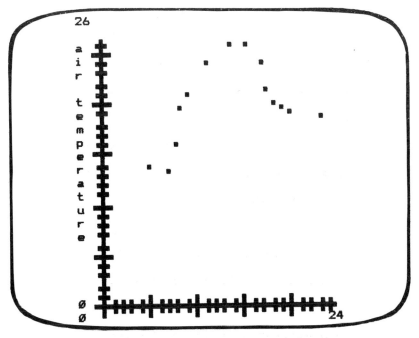

Screen Display 15.2 (second part)

15.9 Activities

i. Enter the following line:

    PRINT CHR$(149);"xyz"

Do block graphics appear on the screen, with the cursor on the next line? Use the cursor control keys in conjunction with the copy key to make a copy of the line of the block graphics. What do they copy as? Can you see why? We discuss this in Section 15.13.

ii. Use the Teletext graphics shown in Table 15.3 to make a composite figure of more than one line. Print your character on the screen and then try to move it continuously from one side of

```
Listing 15.2

10 MODE7
30 PROCclg(4,3)
40 READ end
50 DIM X(end),Y(end)
60 X(0)=end
70 N=0
80 REPEAT
90    N=N+1 :READ X(N),Y(N)
100   UNTIL N=end
110
120 PROCgraph
130 PROCnamey("air temperature")
140 PROCnamex("time of day")
150  REPEAT UNTIL 1=2
160
170 DATA 16,0,0,24,0,5,14,7,13.5,8,16,
    8.25,19.5,9,21,11,24,13.75,25.6
180 DATA 15.25,26,16.75,24,17.25,21.5,
    18,20,19,19.5,20,19.2,23,18.5
```

the screen to the other, as if animated. You will have to remove the old character as well as write up the new one. A space character (ASCII code 32) should help.

15.10 Using the procedures with Teletext

As Teletext facilities offer the full range of colours, and the memory taken up by the screen is only 1K, you will probably want to program various displays in mode 7. With this in mind, we have adapted our procedures for use with Teletext.

The procedures for drawing histograms, pie charts and large, rotated writing proved unsatisfactory in Teletext. Apart from these, all our procedures are available for use with Teletext. Since normal graphics instructions are not available in mode 7, we have also provided several additional procedures:

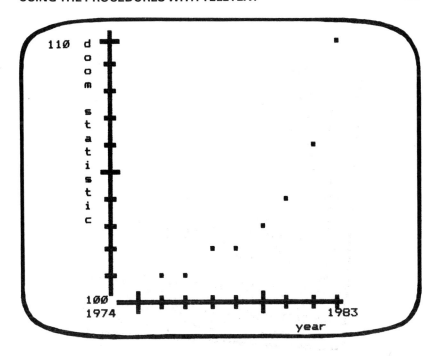

Screen Display 15.3a

PROCclg(B,C) clears the screen and sets the foreground and background colours for graphics. B is the colour number for the background and C is the colour number for the foreground. B must be in the range 0 to 7 and C must be in the range 1 to 7 (see Chapter 2). PROCclg(B,C) must be called before calling any of our other graphics procedures.

PROCdraw(X1,Y1,X2,Y2) draws a line from the point (X1,Y1) to the point (X2,Y2). The range of the co-ordinates is immaterial provided it is within that declared when PROCscale is called.

PROCplot(X,Y) plots a single point at the position X,Y.

For our own use, we saved all the Teletext procedures as a composite which we called TCOMP.

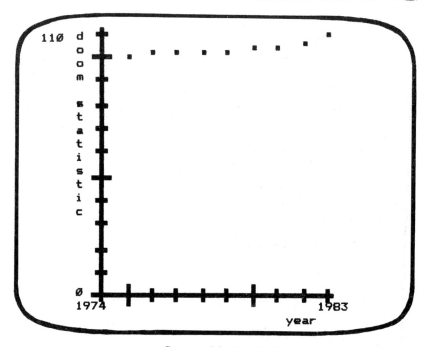

Screen Display 15.3b

Screen Displays 15.1, 15.2, 15.3, 15.4 and 15.5 show the types of display that you can produce with our Teletext procedures. All are Teletext equivalents of Screen Displays that were given earlier, namely Screen Displays 9.1, 9.2, 9.3, 10.1 and 11.1. By comparing them, you can get a good idea of the advantages and disadvantages of programming graphics in mode 7. You will notice that the coarseness of Teletext graphics makes it impossible to graduate the axes entirely uniformly.

15.11 Error messages with Teletext graphics programming

When you come to program in Teletext, having used PROCclg, your programs become impossible to read because they appear largely in Teletext block graphics, rather than in ordinary characters. Although this looks rather strange, it does not affect

```
      Listing 15.3
10 MODE7
20 PRINT ' "This program will display the points"
30 PRINT ' "you provide as co-ordinates, a"
40 PRINT ' "pair at a time. When you are asked for"
50 PRINT ' "the co-ordinates of each point, please"
60 PRINT ' "type the X co-ordinate first, then a"
70 PRINT ' "comma, then the Y co-ordinate. Then"
80 PRINT ' "press RETURN."
90 INPUT ' ' ' "How many points do you want ",N
100 DIM X(N),Y(N)
110 FOR I=1 TO N
120    PRINT ' "Co-ordinates of point ";I;
130    INPUT X(I),Y(I)
140    NEXT I
150 X(0)=N
160 PROCclg(4,3)
170
180 PROCgraph
190 PROCnamey("doom statistic")
200 PROCnamex("year")
220 REPEAT UNTIL 1=2
```

how the programs run. The problem is that any error messages become unreadable too! When you think you have an error message, start by entering the following to clear the screen:

MODE7

Next, enter the following to give the error message in readable characters:

REPORT

Finally, enter the following to get the number of the line responsible for the error:

PRINT ERL

GBM—M

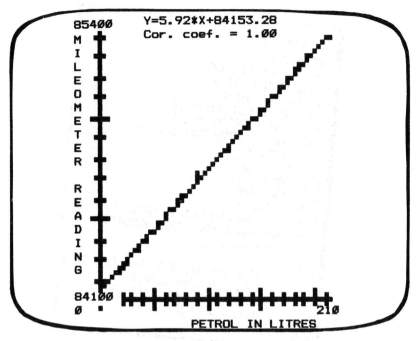

Screen Display 15.4

15.12 Activities

---

i. Experiment with those of our procedures which apply only to Teletext. Do they behave as you expect?

ii. From the earlier chapters, choose one or more of the Screen Displays which rely on the procedures which we provide. Adapt the programs to make them work in Teletext. Do you think that the displays are an improvement?

iii. As Teletext displays can produce more colourful and dramatic displays than those in other modes, you may like to adapt a favourite display of your own for Teletext. Is it an improvement?

```
        Listing 15.4

10 READ N
20 DIM X(N+1),Y(N)
30 X(0)=N :X(1)=0
40 FOR I=1 TO N
50    READ Y(I),X(I+1),S
60    X(I+1)=X(I+1)+X(I)
70    IF I>1 THEN X(I)=X(I)-S
80    NEXT I
90 MODE7
100 PROCclg(4,3)
110 PROCgraph
120 PROCbstln
130 PROCnamex("PETROL IN LITRES")
140 PROCnamey("MILEOMETER READING")
150 REPEAT UNTIL 1=2
160
170    DATA 9 ,84140,30,0 ,84260,20,10 ,
       84442,25,0 ,84612,30,0
180    DATA 84733,20,13 ,84881,30,3 ,
       85060,30,0 ,85231,30,3
190    DATA 85400,30,2
```

15.13 Discussion of activities

Activity 15.5 ii: The two halves of the message are entirely separate. The top half is printed at a fixed position, whereas the lower half moves continuously across the screen.

Activity 15.9i: The new line appears as block graphics because, at its beginning, there is a code for block graphics. Although this is invisible, it is also copied.

This program will draw the shape
produced by any function, provided
it is expressed in BASIC.

Please enter the function when you
see the prompt Y=

Press the space bar when you are
ready to begin.

Enter your equation
Y=EXP(-X/100)*SIN(X/4)

What is the smallest value of X ?0

What is the largest value of X ?9

How many steps?50

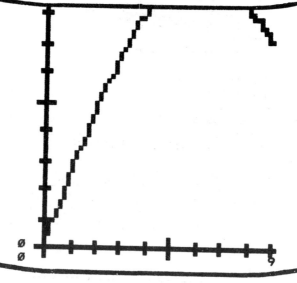

Screen Display 15.5

```
    Listing 15.5
10 MODE7 :VDU 19,0,4;0;19,1,3;0;
20 PRINT ' ' ' '
30 PRINT "This program will draw the shape"
40 PRINT "produced by any function, provided"
50 PRINT "it is expressed in BASIC." '
60 PRINT "Please enter the function when you"
70 PRINT "see the prompt Y="
80 PRINT ' ' "Press the space bar when you are"
90 PRINT "ready to begin." ' '
100 REPEAT UNTIL GET=32
110    INPUT"Enter your equation" ' "Y="A$
120    INPUT ' "What is the smallest value of X ",SX
130    INPUT ' "What is the largest value of X ",LX
140    INPUT ' "How many steps",step%
150
160    DIM X(step%),Y(step%)
170
180    REM Work out largest and smallest Y
190    X=SX:Y(1)=EVAL(A$):Y(2)=Y(1)
200    FOR X=SX TO LX STEP (LX-SX)/step%
210       £Y=EVAL(A$)
220       IFY(2)<£Y THEN Y(2)=£Y
230       IFY(1)>£Y THEN Y(1)=£Y
240       NEXTX
250    X(0)=2 :X(1)=SX :X(2)=LX
260
270    MODE7:PROCclg(4,3)
280    PROCscale
290    PROCaxes
300    PROCgraduate
310    PROCnumber
320    PRINT TAB(5,1);CHR$(130);"Y=";A$
330
340    REM Now display graph
350    X=X(1):LX=FN£CVX(X):LY=FN£CVY(EVAL(A$))
360    FOR X=X(1) TO X(2) STEP (X(2)-X(1))/step%
370       PROCdraw(LX,LY,FN£CVX(X),FN£CVY(EVAL(A$)))
380       LX=FN£CVX(X):LY=FN£CVY(EVAL(A$))
390       NEXTX
400
410    REPEAT UNTIL 1=2
```

Appendix 1
Listings for the procedures

Introduction
The listings
Adaptations of the listings for Teletext

Introduction

This Appendix gives listings of all the procedures. In order to use them, you can either type them in from these listings and store them, or you can buy them ready-recorded on a cassette. If you decide on the former course of action, we recommend that you enter and save each procedure only as you need it. Typing can be quite an arduous job and mistakes are especially likely if too much is taken on at once.

We recommend that you store and use a procedure by first entering it into your computer and then saving it, using the *SPOOL format described in Section 0.2. You need not put in the space after the line number, because the computer will insert it for you, following the LISTO 7 command.

If you have sufficient free memory, it is probably simplest to collect all the procedures which you are likely to use together and to record them as single blocks. For example, for our use, we recorded the procedures in blocks as follows:

TEXT =   PROCchr + PROCmessage + PROCcurve

COMP =   PROCgraph + PROCscale + PROCaxes +
          PROCgraduate + PROCnumber + PROCpoint +
          PROCbstln + PROCnamey + PROCnamex

HISTO =   PROChisto + PROC3Dhisto

PIE =   PROCpie

TCOMP = PROCgraph + PROCscale + PROCaxes +
         PROCgraduate + PROCnumber + PROCpoint +
         PROCbstln + PROCnamey + PROCnamex + PROCclg +
         PROCplot + PROCdraw

This way, when you come to produce a particular type of display, you will know that what you want is available. It is because we expect you to record the procedures together that we have used a different range of line numbers for each one. Then no procedure will normally overwrite another. The exception is for the Teletext procedures. Since you cannot work with Teletext and non-Teletext at the same time, we have purposely arranged for the line numbers of the Teletext procedures to coincide with some of the line numbers of the other procedures. Nevertheless it is probably a good idea to enter NEW before loading the Teletext procedures, if you have just used the non-Teletext ones.

The total memory space of a Model A and a Model B computer in each of the graphics modes is as shown in Table A1.1.

mode	Model A	Model B
7	11776	25342
5	2560	16126
4	2560	16126
2	-	5886
1	-	5886
0	-	5886

Table A1.1

We give the length of each procedure with its listing, so that you can estimate the space that a program will require. The estimate cannot be exact, because it does not only depend on the bytes required for the program and the procedures. It also depends on the bytes required for the numeric variables, the string variables and the arrays.

The listings

PROCchr requires approximately 452 bytes of memory. Its listing is as follows:

```
9000 DEF PROCchr(X,Y,SS,AN,SC)
9010 LOCAL CO1,CO2,SI1,SI2,LX,LY,RX,RY,XX,YY
9020 CO1=COS(AN):SI1=-SIN(AN)
9030 CO2=COS(PI/2-AN):SI2=SIN(AN+PI/2)
9040 £F=£F+1:IF £F=1 THEN DIM M 8 ELSE £F=2
9050 A%=10:X%=M MOD256:Y%=M DIV256:?M=ASC(S$):CALL(&FFF1)
9060 FOR XX=0TO7 :FOR YY=0TO7
9070   IF ?(M+8-YY) AND 2^(7-XX) THEN PROCpixel
9080   NEXT YY,XX
9090 ENDPROC
9100 DEF PROCpixel
9110 LX=XX-.5:RX=XX+.5:LY=YY-.5:RY=YY+.5
9120 MOVE X+SC*(LX*CO1+LY*SI1),Y+SC*(LY*SI2+LX*CO2)
9130 MOVE X+SC*(RX*CO1+LY*SI1),Y+SC*(LY*SI2+RX*CO2)
9140 PLOT 85,X+SC*(LX*CO1+RY*SI1),Y+SC*(RY*SI2+LX*CO2)
9150 PLOT 85,X+SC*(RX*CO1+RY*SI1),Y+SC*(RY*SI2+RX*CO2)
9160 ENDPROC
```

PROCmessage requires approximately 171 bytes of memory. Its listing is as follows:

```
9180 DEFPROCmessage(X,Y,S$,AN,SC)
9190 LOCAL I,XP,YP
9200 AN=AN+PI/2
9210 FOR I=1 TO LEN(S$)
9220   XP=SC*(COS(AN)*8*(I-1))
9230   YP=SC*(SIN(AN)*8*(I-1))
9240   PROCchr(X+XP,Y+YP,MID$(S$,I,1),AN,SC)
9250   NEXT I
9260 ENDPROC
```

PROCcurve requires approximately 238 bytes of memory. Its listing is as follows:

```
9280 DEFPROCcurve(X,Y,R,SA,FA,S$,SC)
9290 LOCAL I,XP,YP
9300 SA=SA+PI/2:FA=FA+PI/2
```

```
9310 FOR I=1 TO LEN(S$)
9320   XP=X+R*COS(SA-(SA-FA)*(I-1)/(LEN(S$)+1))
9330   YP=Y+R*SIN(SA-(SA-FA)*(I-1)/(LEN(S$)+1))
9340   PROCchr(XP,YP,MID$(S$,I,1),SA-(SA-FA)*(I-1)/
       (LEN(S$)+1)-PI/2,SC)
9350   NEXT I
9360 ENDPROC
```

PROCgraph requires approximately 132 bytes of memory. Its listing is as follows:

```
10000 DEF PROCgraph
10010 PROCscale
10020 PROCaxes
10030 PROCgraduate
10040 PROCnumber
10050 FOR £J=1 TO X(0)
10060   DTA=8 :PROCpoint(X(£J),Y(£J))
10070   NEXT £J
10080 ENDPROC
```

PROCscale requires approximately 943 bytes of memory. Its listing is as follows:

```
10100 DEF PROCscale
10110 £SX=X(1) :£LX=£SX :£SY=Y(1) :£LY=£SY
10120 FOR £I=1 TO X(0)
10130   IF£SX>X(£I)THEN£SX=X(£I)
10140   IF£LX<X(£I)THEN£LX=X(£I)
10150   IF£SY>Y(£I)THEN£SY=Y(£I)
10160   IF£LY<Y(£I)THEN£LY=Y(£I)
10170   NEXT
10180 PROCscale2(£SY,£LY) :£SY=£S :£LY=£L
      :£STY=£ST :£CBY%=£CBN%
10190 PROCscale2(£SX,£LX) :£SX=£S :£LX=£L
      :£STX=£ST :£CBX%=£CBN%
10200 £X=1000/(£LX-£SX):£Y=800/(£LY-£SY)
10210 £CONVX=150-£SX*£X :£CONVY=100-£SY*£Y
10220 ENDPROC
10230 :
10240 DEF FN£CVX(G) =£X*G+£CONVX
10250 DEF FN£CVY(G) =£Y*G+£CONVY
10260 :
10270 DEF PROCscale2(L,H) :@%=&0101090A
```

```
10280 IF L>0 AND L<H/3 THEN L=0 ELSE IF H<0 AND
      H>L/3 THEN H=0
10290 £LL=VAL(LEFT$(STR$(L),INSTR(STR$(L),"E")-1))
10300 £LH=VAL(LEFT$(STR$(H),INSTR(STR$(H),"E")-1))
10310 £PL=VAL(MID$(STR$(L),INSTR(STR$(L),"E")+1))
10320 £LH=£LH*10^(VAL(MID$(STR$(H),INSTR(STR$(H),"E")+
      1))-£PL)
10330 £D=£LH-£LL
10340 IF £D<=3THENREPEAT£D=£D*10 :£PL=£PL-1 :£LL=£LL*10
      :£LH=£LH*10 :UNTIL £D>3
10350 IF £D>30THENREPEAT£D=£D/10 :£PL=£PL+1 :£LL=£LL/10
      :£LH=£LH/10 :UNTIL £D<30
10360 £LL=INT(£LL+.1) :£LH=INT(£LH+.5)
10370 @%=&10 :£CBN%=SGN(£LL)*(VAL(RIGHT$(STR$(£LL),1))+.1)
10380 £S=VAL(STR$(£LL)+"E"+STR$(£PL))
10390 £L=VAL(STR$(£LH)+"E"+STR$(£PL)) :£ST=ABS(£L-£S)/
      (£LH-£LL)
10400 ENDPROC
```

PROCaxes requires approximately 223 bytes of memory. Its listing is as follows:

```
10420 DEF PROCaxes
10430 £X0=0 :£Y0=0
10440 IF £SX>0 THEN £X0=£SX ELSE IF £LX<0 THEN £X0=£LX
10450 IF £SY>0 THEN £Y0=£SY ELSE IF £LY<0 THEN £Y0=£LY
10460 MOVE FN£CVX(£SX),FN£CVY(£Y0) :DRAW FN£CVX(£LX),
      FN£CVY(£Y0)
10470 MOVE FN£CVX(£X0),FN£CVY(£SY) :DRAW FN£CVX(£X0),
      FN£CVY(£LY)
10480 ENDPROC
```

PROCgraduate requires approximately 228 bytes of memory. Its listing is as follows:

```
10500 DEF PROCgraduate
10510 FOR x=£SX TO £LX+.1*£STX STEP £STX
10520    IF £CBX%MOD5=0 THEN DTA=16 ELSE DTA=8
10530    £CBX%=£CBX%+1 :PROCpoint(x,£Y0) :NEXT x
10540 FOR y=£SY TO £LY+.1*£STY STEP £STY
10550    IF £CBY%MOD5=0 THEN DTA=16 ELSE DTA=8
10560    £CBY%=£CBY%+1 :PROCpoint(£X0,y) :NEXT y
10570 ENDPROC
```

PROCnumber requires approximately 225 bytes of memory. Its listing is as follows:

```
10590 DEF PROCnumber :VDU5
10600 MOVE FN£CVX(£LX)-4*LEN(STR$(£LX)),FN£CVY(£Y0)-20
      :PRINT;£LX
10610 MOVEFN£CVX(£X0)-150,FN£CVY(£LY)+28:PRINT;£LY
10620 IF £LX>0AND£SX<0AND£LY>0AND£SY<0THEN ENDPROC
10630 MOVE FN£CVX(£SX),FN£CVY(£Y0)-20:PRINT;£SX
10640 MOVEFN£CVX(£X0)-150,FN£CVY(£SY)+30:PRINT;£SY:VDU4
10650 ENDPROC
```

PROCpoint requires approximately 127 bytes of memory. Its listing is as follows:

```
10670 DEF PROCpoint(A,B)
10680   MOVEFN£CVX(A)-DTA,FN£CVY(B):DRAWFN£CVX(A)+DTA,
        FN£CVY(B)
10690 MOVEFN£CVX(A),FN£CVY(B)-DTA :DRAWFN£CVX(A),FN£CVY(B)
      +DTA
10700 ENDPROC
```

PROCbstln requires approximately 733 bytes of memory. Its listing is as follows:

```
10720 DEF PROCbstln
10730 LOCAL C,M,I,XX,YY,MEANX,MEANY,sumX,sumY,sumXY,sumYY,
      sumXX,MINX,MAXX,XY
10740 XX=0 :YY=0: XY=0: sumX=0: sum Y=0
10750 FOR I=1 TO X(0) :sumX=sumX+X(I) :sumY=sumY+Y(I)
      :NEXT I
10760 MEANX=sumX/X(0) :MEANY=sumY/X(0)
10770 MINX=X(1):MAXX=MINX:sumXX=0:sumYY=0:sumXY=0
10780 FOR I=1 TO X(0)
10790   sumXX=sumXX+X(I)*X(I) :sumYY=sumYY+Y(I)*Y(I)
10800   sumXY=sumXY+X(I)*Y(I)
10810   XX=XX+(X(I)-MEANX)^2 :YY=YY+(Y(I)-MEANY)^2 :XY=XY+
        (X(I)-MEANX)*(Y(I)-MEANY)
10820   IF MINX>X(I) THEN MINX=X(I)
10830   IF MAXX<X(I) THEN MAXX=X(I)
10840   NEXT I
10850 M=(X(0)*sumXY-sumX*sumY)/(X(0)*sumXX-sumX*sumX)
```

```
10860 C=(sumY*sumXX-sumX*sumXY)/(X(0)*sumXX-sumX*sumX)
10870 @%=&20204 :VDU4
10880 PRINT TAB(10,0);"Y=";M;"*X+";C;TAB(10,1);"Cor.
      coef. = ";XY/SQR(XX*YY)
10890 MOVE FN£CVX(£SX),FN£CVY(M*£SX+C) :DRAW FN£CVX(£LX),
      FN£CVY(M*£LX+C)
10900 @%=&10 :ENDPROC
```

PROCnamey requires approximately 124 bytes of memory. Its
listing is as follows:

```
10920 DEF PROCnamey(£Vname$):VDU5
10930 FOR £A=1 TO LEN(£Vname$)
10940   MOVE FN£CVX(£X0)-60,FN£CVY(£LY)-£A*32-32
        :PRINTMID$(£Vname$,£A,1)
10950   NEXT £A:VDU4
10960 ENDPROC
```

PROCnamex requires approximately 93 bytes of memory. Its
listing is as follows:

```
10980 DEF PROCnamex(£Hname$)
10990 MOVE FN£CVX(£LX)-32*LEN(£Hname$)-64,FN£CVY(£Y0)-52
      :VDU5:PRINT£Hname$:VDU4
11000 ENDPROC
```

PROChisto requires approximately 285 bytes of memory. Its
listing is as follows:

```
12000 DEF PROChisto
12010 £C=1
12020 FOR £A=1 TO X(0)-1
12030   GCOL0,£C :£C=£C+1 :IF £C>2 THEN £C=1
12040   £XL=FN£CVX(X(£A)-£IN) :£XR=FN£CVX(X(£A))
12050   £YH=FN£CVY(Y(£A))
12060   £YB=FN£CVY(0)
12070   MOVE £XL,£YB :MOVE £XL,£YH
12080   PLOT 85,£XR,£YB :PLOT 85,£XR,£YH
12090   GCOL 0,3
12100   MOVE £XL,£YB :DRAW £XR,£YB
12110   DRAW £XR,£YH :DRAW £XL,£YH :DRAW £XL,£YB
12120   NEXT £A
12130 ENDPROC
```

PROC3Dhisto requires approximately 459 bytes of memory. Its listing is as follows:

```
12150 DEF PROC3Dhisto(C)
12160 FOR £A=1 TO X(0)-1
12170    £XL=FN£CVX(X(£A)-£IN) :£XR=FN£CVX(X(£A))
12180    £YB=FN£CVY(0) :£YH=FN£CVY(Y(£A))
12190    GCOL 0,C
12200    MOVE £XL,£YB :MOVE £XL,£YH
12210    PLOT 85,£XR,£YB :PLOT 85,£XR,£YH
12220    GCOL 0,3-C
12230    PLOT 85,£XR+64,£YB+32
12240    PLOT 85,£XR+64,£YH+32
12250    MOVE £XR,£YH
12260    PLOT 85,£XL+64,£YH+32
12270    PLOT 85,£XL,£YH
12280    GCOL 0,3
12290    MOVE £XL,£YH:DRAW £XL+64,£YH+32
12300    DRAW £XR+64,£YH+32
12310    DRAW £XR,£YH:DRAW £XL,£YH
12320    DRAW £XL,£YB:DRAW £XR,£YB
12330    DRAW £XR,£YH:DRAW £XR+64,£YH+32
12340    DRAW £XR+64,£YB+32:DRAW£XR,£YB
12350    NEXT £A
12360 ENDPROC
```

PROCpie requires approximately 598 bytes of memory. Its listing is as follows:

```
13000 DEF PROCpie(R%,X%,Y%,T)
13010 LOCAL L%,S,W
13020 W=0:S=0:C%=0
13030 FOR L%=1 TO £NS
13040    W=W+£S(L%)
13050    C%=C%+1:IFC%>2THENC%=1
13060    IFL%=£NS THENC%=3
13070    PROCsector(C%,S/T,W/T,R%,X%,Y%)
13080    S=W
13090    NEXTL%
13100 PROClabel(R%,X%,Y%,T)
13110 ENDPROC
13120 :
```

```
13130 DEF PROCsector(C%,S,F,R%,X%,Y%)
13140 LOCAL L
13150 GCOL0,C%
13160 MOVE COS(2*PI*S)*R%+X%,SIN(2*PI*S)*R%+Y%
13170 FOR L= 2*PI*S TO 2*PI*F STEP 0.1
13180    MOVE X%,Y%
13190    PLOT 85,COS(L)*R%+X%,SIN(L)*R%+Y%
13200    NEXTL
13210 PLOT85,COS(2*PI*F)*R%+X%,SIN(2*PI*F)*R%+Y%
13220 ENDPROC
13230 :
13240 DEF PROClabel(R%,X%,Y%,T)
13250 VDU5:B=0:R%=R%+64
13260 FOR A=1 TO £NS
13270    OX=0:H=(B+£S(A)/2)*2*PI/T
13280    IFH<PI*1.5 ANDH>PI*.5 THENOX=-(LEN(£N$(A)))*32)
13290    MOVE COS(H)*R%+X%+OX,SIN(H)*R%+Y%
13300    PRINT£N$(A)
13310    B=B+£S(A)
13320    NEXTA
13330 VDU4
13340 ENDPROC
```

Adaptations of the listings for Teletext

PROCgraph requires approximately 132 bytes of memory. Its listing is as follows:

```
10000 DEF PROCgraph
10010 PROCscale
10020 PROCaxes
10030 PROCgraduate
10040 PROCnumber
10050 FOR £J=1 TO X(0)
10060    PROCplot(FN£CVX(X(£J)),FN£CVY(Y(£J)))
10070    NEXT £J
10080 ENDPROC
```

PROCscale requires approximately 967 bytes of memory. Its listing is as follows:

```
10100 DEF PROCscale
10110 £SX=X(1) :£LX=£SX :£SY=Y(1) :£LY=£SY
10120 FOR £I=1 TO X(0)
10130   IF£SX>X(£I)THEN£SX=X(£I)
10140   IF£LX<X(£I)THEN£LX=X(£I)
10150   IF£SY>Y(£I)THEN£SY=Y(£I)
10160   IF£LY<Y(£I)THEN£LY=Y(£I)
10170   NEXT
10180 PROCscale2(£SX,£LX) :£SX=£S :£LX=£L :£STX=£ST
      :£CBX%=£CBN%
10190 PROCscale2(£SY,£LY) :£SY=£S :£LY=£L :£STY=£ST
      :£CBY%=£CBN%
10200 £X=1000/(£LX-£SX):£Y=800/(£LY-£SY)
10210 £CONVX=150-£SX*£X :£CONVY=100-£SY*£Y
10220 ENDPROC
10230 :
10240 DEF FN£CVX(G) =INT((£X*G+£CONVX)*74/1280)
10250 DEF FN£CVY(G) =INT((£Y*G+£CONVY)*75/1024)
10260 :
10270 DEF PROCscale2(L,H) :@%=&0101090A
10280 IF L>0 AND L<H/3 THEN L=0 ELSE IF H<0 AND H>L/3
      THEN H=0
10290 £LL=VAL(LEFT$(STR$(L),INSTR(STR$(L),"E")-1))
10300 £LH=VAL(LEFT$(STR$(H),INSTR(STR$(H),"E")-1))
10310 £PL=VAL(MID$(STR$(L),INSTR(STR$(L),"E")+1))
10320 £LH=£LH*10^(VAL(MID$(STR$(H),INSTR(STR$(H),"E")+
      1))-£PL)
10330 £D=£LH-£LL
10340 IF £D<=3THENREPEAT£D=£D*10 :£PL=£PL-1 :£LL=£LL*10
      :£LH=£LH*10 :UNTIL£D>3
10350 IF £D>30THENREPEAT£D=£D/10 :£PL=£PL+1 :£LL=£LL/10
      :£LH=£LH/10 :UNTIL£D<30
10360 £LL=INT(£LL+.1) :£LH=INT(£LH+.5)
10370 @%=&10 :£CBN%=SGN(£LL)*(VAL(RIGHT$(STR$(£LL),1))+.1)
10380 £S=VAL(STR$(£LL)+"E"+STR$(£PL))
10390 £L=VAL(STR$(£LH)+"E"+STR$(£PL)) :£ST=ABS(£L-£S)/
      (£LH-£LL)
10400 ENDPROC
```

PROCaxes requires approximately 231 bytes of memory. Its listing is as follows:

```
10420 DEF PROCaxes
10430 £X0=0 :£Y0=0
10440 IF £SX>0 THEN £X0=£SX ELSE IF £LX<0 THEN £X0=£LX
10450 IF £SY>0 THEN £Y0=£SY ELSE IF £LY<0 THEN £Y0=£LY
10460 PROCdraw(FN£CVX(£SX),FN£CVY(£Y0),FN£CVX(£LX),
      FN£CVY(£Y0))
10470 PROCdraw(FN£CVX(£X0),FN£CVY(£SY),FN£CVX(£X0),
      FN£CVY(£LY))
10480 ENDPROC
```

PROCgraduate requires approximately 227 bytes of memory. Its listing is as follows:

```
10500 DEF PROCgraduate
10510 FOR x=£SX TO £LX+.1*£STX STEP £STX
10520    IF £CBX%MOD5=0 THEN DTA=2 ELSE DTA=1
10530    £CBX%=£CBX%+1 :PROCpoint(x,£Y0) :NEXT x
10540 FOR y=£SY TO £LY+.1*£STY STEP £STY
10550    IF £CBY%MOD5=0 THEN DTA=2 ELSE DTA=1
10560    £CBY%=£CBY%+1 :PROCpoint(£X0,y) :NEXT y
10570 ENDPROC
```

PROCnumber requires approximately 292 bytes of memory. Its listing is as follows:

```
10590 DEF PROCnumber
10600 PROCplot(FN£CVX(£LX)-LEN(STR$(£LX)),FN£CVY(£Y0)-3)
      :PRINTCHR$127;CHR$134;£LX;CHR$147;
10610 PROCplot(FN£CVX(£X0)-7,FN£CVY(£LY)+4):
      PRINTCHR$127;CHR$134;£LY;CHR$147;
10620 IF £LX>0AND£SX<0AND£LY>0AND£SY<0 THEN ENDPROC
10630 PROCplot(FN£CVX(£SX)-7,FN£CVY(£Y0)-3):
      PRINTCHR$127;CHR$134;£SX;CHR$147;
10640 PROCplot(FN£CVX(£X0)-7,FN£CVY(£SY)):
      PRINTCHR$127;CHR$134;£SY;CHR$147;
10650 ENDPROC
```

PROCpoint requires approximately 135 bytes of memory. Its listing is as follows:

```
10670 DEF PROCpoint(A,B)
10680 PROCdraw(FN£CVX(A)-DTA,FN£CVY(B),FN£CVX(A)+DTA,
      FN£CVY(B))
10690 PROCdraw(FN£CVX(A),FN£CVY(B)-DTA,FN£CVX(A),
      FN£CVY(B)+DTA)
10700 ENDPROC
```

PROCbstln requires approximately 384 bytes of memory. Its listing is as follows:

```
10720 DEF PROCbstln
10730 LOCAL C,M,I,XX,YY,MEANX,MEANY,sumX,sumY,sumXY,
      sumYY,sumXX,MINX,MAXX,XY
10740 XX=Ø :YY=Ø
10750 FOR I=1 TO X(Ø)
10760   XX=XX+X(I) : YY=YY+Y(I)
10770   NEXT I
10780 MEANX=XX/X(Ø) :MEANY=YY/X(Ø)
10790 MINX=X(1):MAXX=MINX:sumX=Ø:sumY=Ø:sumXX=Ø
      :sumYY=Ø:sumXY=Ø:XX=Ø:YY=Ø :XY=Ø
10800 FOR I=1 TO X(Ø)
10810   sumX=sumX+X(I)  :sumXX=sumXX+X(I)*X(I)
10820   sumY=sumY+Y(I)  :sumYY=sumYY+Y(I)*Y(I)
10830   sumXY=sumXY+X(I)*Y(I)
10840   XX=XX+(X(I)-MEANX)^2 :YY=YY+(Y(I)-MEANY)^2
      :XY=XY+(X(I)-MEANX)*(Y(I)-MEANY)
10850   IF MINX>X(I) THEN MINX=X(I)
10860   IF MAXX<X(I) THEN MAXX=X(I)
10870   NEXT I
10880 M=(X(Ø)*sumXY-sumX*sumY)/(X(Ø)*sumXX-sumX*sumX)
10890 C=(sumY*sumXX-sumX*sumXY)/(X(Ø)*sumXX-sumX*sumX)
10900 @%=&20204
10910 PRINT TAB(9,Ø);CHR$135;"Y=";M;"*X+";C;CHR$147;TAB(
      9,1);CHR$135;"Cor. coef. = ";XY/SQR(XX*YY);CHR$147
10920 PROCdraw(FN£CVX(£SX),FN£CVY(M*£SX+C),FN£CVX(£LX),
      FN£CVY(M*£LX+C))
10930 @%=10:ENDPROC
```

PROCnamey requires approximately 135 bytes of memory. Its listing is as follows:

```
10950 DEF PROCnamey(£Vname$)
10960 FOR £A=1 TO LEN(£Vname$)
10970    PROCplot(FN£CVX(£X0)-8,FN£CVY(£LY)-£A*3+3):PRINT
         CHR$127;CHR$135;MID$(£Vname$,£A,1);CHR$147;
10980    NEXT £A
10990 ENDPROC
```

PROCnamex requires approximately 104 bytes of memory. Its listing is as follows:

```
11010 DEF PROCnamex(£Hname$)
11020 PROCplot(FN£CVX(£LX)-2*LEN(£Hname$)-3,
      FN£CVY(£Y0)-6):VDU127,135:PRINT£Hname$;CHR$147;
11030 ENDPROC
```

PROCclg requires approximately 227 bytes of memory. Its listing is as follows:

```
11050 DEFPROCclg(C,G)
11060 VDU 28,0,24,39,0,23,0,10,32;0;0;0;
11070 LOCAL CH,GH,Y
11080 CH=128+C : CLS
11090 IF C<1 OR C>7 THEN CH=132
11100 GH=144+G
11110 IF G<1 OR G>7 THEN GH=156
11120 FOR Y=0 TO 24
11130    PRINT TAB(0,Y);
11140    VDU CH,157,GH
11150    NEXT Y
11160 VDU 28,3,24,39,0
11170 PRINT TAB(0,0);
11180 ENDPROC
```

PROCplot requires approximately 212 bytes of memory. Its listing is as follows:

```
11200 DEFPROCplot(X,Y)
11210 IF X>73 OR X<0 THEN ENDPROC
11220 IF Y>74 OR Y<0 THEN ENDPROC
11230 LOCAL A%,C%
11240 PRINT TAB(X DIV 2,24-Y DIV 3);
11250 C%=(X AND1)+(Y MOD3)*2
11260 C%=VAL(MID$("166404080102",C%*2+1,2))
11270 A%=135
11280 VDU (USR &FFF4 AND &FF00) DIV 256 OR C% OR 128
11290 ENDPROC
```

PROCdraw requires approximately 189 bytes of memory. Its listing is as follows:

```
11310 DEFPROCdraw(X1,Y1,X2,Y2)
11320 PROCplot(X1,Y1) :PROCplot(X2,Y2)
11330 LOCAL X,Y,L,A
11340 X=(X2-X1) :Y=(Y2-Y1)
11350 L=SQR((X1-X2)^2+(Y1-Y2)^2)
11360 FOR A=1 TO L
11370    IF L<>0 THEN PROCplot(X1+A*X/L,Y1+A*Y/L)
11380    NEXT A
11390 ENDPROC
```

Appendix 2
How the procedures work

This appendix explains how each of the procedures works. For simplicity, a horizontal and a vertical axis is referred to as an x and a y axis, respectively; and co-ordinates are referred to as x and y co-ordinates.

THE PROCEDURE PROCscale

PROCscale scales any display so that it squarely fills the screen, irrespective of the magnitude and range of the data. This frees you from having to consider such things as screen co-ordinates and addressable points, etc.

PROCscale requires $X(0)$ to hold the number of points to be plotted, and the arrays $X()$ and $Y()$ to hold the x and y co-ordinates for these points. There must be a minimum of two X values in $X(1)$ and $X(2)$ and two Y values in $Y(1)$ and $Y(2)$. Neither set of co-ordinates can cover a zero range. For example, although you could plot a graph consisting of a single vertical or horizontal line, the axes must cover a finite range.

PROCscale examines the numbers in the arrays and then sets up the scaling for the other procedures to follow. It must therefore be called before any of the following are called:

PROCaxes	PROCgraduate	PROCnumber
PROCpoint	PROCgraph	PROCnamex
PROCnamey	PROCbstsl	PROChist
PROC3Dhisto		

PROCscale gives values to the following variables:

i. £SX is set to the smallest x value, rounded to the nearest left-most graduation on any axes.
ii. £LX is set to the largest x value, rounded to the nearest right-most graduation on any axes.
iii. £SY, £LY set the y values in the same way as the x values.
iv. £D sets the number of divisions along the x axis.
v. £ST is set, in the user's own co-ordinates, to the increment corresponding to one scale division along the x axis.

The operation of PROCscale: smallest and largest values

The first set of lines in PROCscale merely find the smallest and largest values available in the X() and Y() arrays. Line 10100 defines the procedure name. Line 10110 sets the initial values for the smallest and largest X and Y values, and line 10120 sets up a FOR ... NEXT loop. When these lines have been executed, the smallest and largest x values are held in £SX and £LX, and the smallest and largest y values are held in £SY and £LY. These lines are reproduced below so that you can easily refer to them.

```
10100 DEF PROCscale
10110 £SX=X(1) :£LX=£SX :£SY=Y(1) :£LY=£SY
10120 FOR £I=1 TO X(Ø)
10130     IF£SX>X(£I)THEN£SX=X(£I)
10140     IF£LX<X(£I)THEN£LX=X(£I)
10150     IF£SY>Y(£I)THEN£SY=Y(£I)
10160     IF£LY<Y(£I)THEN£LY=Y(£I)
10170     NEXT
```

The operation of PROCscale: co-ordinates for the ends of the axes.

The smallest and largest values, as determined by the lines 10120 to 10170, will not normally be ideal values for the ends of the axes. For example, if the smallest and largest value for one axis are 0.1 and 9.3 respectively, then the axis would clearly be best running from 0 to 10. PROCscale contains a sub-procedure, PROCscale2 (discussed later), which makes this sort of decision. Lines 10180 and 10190 call on it, to set the ideal end points for the axes, first for the y axis and then for the x. They work by assigning new values for £SX, £SY etc.

```
10180 PROCscale2(£SY,£LY) :£SY=£S :£LY=£L
      :£STY=£ST :£CBY%=£CBN%
10190 PROCscale2(£SX,£LX) :£SX=£S :£LX=£L
      :£STX=£ST :£CBX%=£CBN%
```

The sub-procedure also calculates the step size £ST and a quantity £CBN% which is used to locate every fifth scale division. This division is marked larger than the others by PROCgraduate, to make it easier to read from the axes.

The operation of PROCscale: conversion to screen co-ordinates

The final task of PROCscale is to work out some of the constants which will be required in order to calculate the screen co-ordinates from co-ordinates which are supplied by the user. For these calculations we set the screen area for graphics to a rectangle with 150,100 as the lower left-hand co-ordinate. This area extends 1000 screen co-ordinates horizontally and 800 vertically. These numbers appear in lines 10200 and 10210 which are reproduced below for easy reference. Altering these numbers, alters the area of the screen used for the graphics.

Line 10200 calculates the important scale factors £X and £Y. These are the factors by which the x and y values supplied by the user must be multiplied, so as to bring them into the range of the screen co-ordinates.

Line 10210 adds an offset to prevent the graphics extending down to the bottom left-hand corner of the screen.

```
10200 £X=1000/(£LX-£SX):£Y=800/(£LY-£SY)
10210 £CONVX=150-£SX*£X :£CONVY=100-£SY*£Y
10220 ENDPROC
```

The operation of PROCscale: the convert functions

The procedure sets up two important functions FN£CVX and FN£CVY which convert from the x and y values supplied by the user to those required by the computer's plotting routines. Lines 10240 and 10250 below define these functions, using the scale factors and offset set up by lines 10200 and 10210.

```
10240 DEF FN£CVX(G) =£X*G+£CONVX
10250 DEF FN£CVY(G) =£Y*G+£CONVY
```

The operation of PROCscale: PROCscale2

PROCscale2 is a part of PROCscale. For convenience of programming, it was written as a separate procedure, but there would be no sense in calling it from within a program.
The following few sections explain how PROCscale2 works.

The operation of PROCscale2: number formats

PROCscale2 relies on the BBC Microcomputer's ability to dictate the format of numbers. The format specification is made initially in line 10270 using @%=&0101090A. This dicatates not only the printed format of numbers but, more importantly for our purpose, the format of any number converted to a string using the STR$ function. Line 10290 is an example.

```
10270 DEF PROCscale2(L,H)  :@%=&0101090A
```

The operation of PROCscale2: the choice of origin

It is invariably preferable for a display to include the origin, provided that the graph is not consequently cramped up on one side. The first decision which PROCscale2 makes is in line 10280 and concerns whether the origin should be included in the display. For a graph which shows only positive numbers, our condition is simply (and arbitrarily) that if the smallest number is less than 1/3 of the largest, then the origin should be included. Line 10280 expresses this condition. Without it, there would be no criterion for the inclusion of the origin.

```
10280 IF L>0 AND L<H/3 THEN L=0 ELSE IF H<0 AND
      H>L/3 THEN H=0
```

The operation of PROCscale2: the number of graduations

Lines 10290, 10300, 10310 and 10320 take the smallest and largest numbers supplied to the procedure and convert them to a decimal fraction and an exponent. The decimal fraction is held in £LL and £LH while the exponent is held in £PL.

```
10290 £LL=VAL(LEFT$(STR$(L),INSTR(STR$(L),"E")-1))
10300 £LH=VAL(LEFT$(STR$(H),INSTR(STR$(H),"E")-1))
```

```
10310  £PL=VAL(MID$(STR$(L),INSTR(STR$(L),"E")+1))
10320  £LH=£LH*10^(VAL(MID$(STR$(H),INSTR(STR$(H),"E")+
       1))-£PL)
```

It might be best to illustrate what is happening so far with an example. Suppose that the x axis is being considered and that the user's program has supplied the smallest and largest numbers as 0.01 and 0.0145. Lines 10290 to 10320 will convert these values to 1.0 E-2 and 1.45 E-2. The 1.0 and 1.45 will be held in the variables £LL and £LH respectively with -2 held in £PL.

The next few lines now make the decision as to how many divisions should be along the axis. The variable £D holds the number of divisions which are initially set to the difference between £LH and £LL.

```
10330  £D=£LH-£LL
```

Then the two lines 10340 and 10350 multiply up or divide down this difference until it is in the range 4 to 30 inclusive. When multiplying or dividing by ten, these lines also alter the exponent held in £PL to keep track of the magnitude of the number.

```
10340  IF £D<=3THENREPEAT£D=£D*10 :£PL=£PL-1 :£LL=£LL*10
       :£LH=£LH*10 :UNTIL £D>3
10350  IF £D>30THENREPEAT£D=£D/10 :£PL=£PL+1 :£LL=£LL/10
       :£LH=£LH/10 :UNTIL £D<30
```

Before these lines are executed, the £D in our example would have an initial value of 0.45. The condition in line 10340 would result in the value of £D being multiplied by ten and the other values being accordingly adjusted to give £LL=10, £LH=14.5 and £D=4.5.

The operation of PROCscale2: values for the ends of the axes

The next line sets the values of £LL and £LH to integer values rounding £LL down and £LH up. This is necessary in order for the scale along the axes to start and finish at sensible numbers.

```
10360  £LL=INT(£LL+.1) :£LH=INT(£LH+.5)
```

For our example numbers, this would set £LL to 10 and £LH to 15 for an eventual range along the axes from 0.01 to 0.015. This nicely encompasses the original range of numbers from 0.01 to 0.0145.

The operation of PROCscale2: the guide to every fifth graduation

The next line picks off the least significant digit of £LL and stores it in £CBN%, as a guide to the graduation procedure when to draw larger graduations every fifth position. With our example figures, this sets £CBN% equal to 0. It also resets the format for presenting numbers.

```
10370 @%=&10 :£CBN%=SGN(£LL)*(VAL(RIGHT$(STR$(£LL),1))+.1)
```

The operation of PROCscale2: the smallest and largest values

The last two lines of this procedure then place the smallest and largest numbers represented by the recommended scale in £S and £L.

```
10380 £S=VAL(STR$(£LL)+"E"+STR$(£PL))
10390 £L=VAL(STR$(£LH)+"E"+STR$(£PL))  :£ST=ABS(£L-£S)/
      (£LH-£LL)
10400 ENDPROC
```

THE PROCEDURE PROCaxes

PROCaxes draws a pair of axes i.e. an x axis and a y axis.

The operation of PROCaxes: the origin

Axes do not necessarily cross at the origin. Lines 10440 and 10450 examine the range of the values along the axes and accordingly set where the axes should cross in order to make the best display.

Line 10460 draws the x axis and line 10470 draws the Y axis.

```
10420 DEF PROCaxes
10430 £X0=0 :£Y0=0
10440 IF £SX>0 THEN £X0=£SX ELSE IF £LX<0 THEN £X0=£LX
10450 IF £SY>0 THEN £Y0=£SY ELSE IF £LY<0 THEN £Y0=£LY
10460 MOVE FN£CVX(£SX),FN£CVY(£Y0) :DRAW FN£CVX(£LX),
      FN£CVY(£Y0)
10470 MOVE FN£CVX(£X0),FN£CVY(£SY) :DRAW FN£CVX(£X0),
      FN£CVY(£LY)
10480 ENDPROC
```

THE PROCEDURE PROCgraduate

PROCgraduate marks off the axes into appropriate intervals:
never less than four or more than 30 graduations along each axis.

The operation of PROCgraduate: the graduations

To make it easier to read values from the graphs, every fifth
graduation is made larger than the rest. PROCgraduate is in two
parts, one for the x axis and one for the y. A FOR...NEXT loop
steps along each axis from the smallest value to the largest with
a step size £STX fixed by PROCscale. In lines 10510 and 10540
the end of the FOR...NEXT loop is set slightly larger than might
seem necessary. Without this, there would be some occasions
when one less graduation than expected would be drawn. As
PROCpoint actually draws a small + sign, it is equally suitable
for plotting points and for marking both axes. So the call to
PROCpoint in lines 10530 and 10560 actually draws the
graduations.

The operation of PROCgraduate: every fifth graduation

The length of the bars of the + sign is controlled by the constant
DTA. Examination of £CBX% or £CBY% in lines 10520 and 10550
makes the bars extra large when every fifth division is reached.

```
10500 DEF PROCgraduate
10510 FOR x=£SX TO £LX+.1*£STX STEP £STX
10520    IF £CBX%MOD5=0 THEN DTA=16 ELSE DTA=8
```

```
10530 £CBX%=£CBX%+1 :PROCpoint(x,£Y0) :NEXT x
10540 FOR y=£SY TO £LY+.1*£STY STEP £STY
10550   IF £CBY%MOD5=0 THEN DTA=16 ELSE DTA=8
10560   £CBY%=£CBY%+1 :PROCpoint(£X0,y) :NEXT y
10570 ENDPROC
```

THE PROCEDURE PROCnumber

PROCnumber prints a number against the first and last scale division of each axis to indicate the scale.

The operation of PROCnumber: the location of the numbers

The numbers are located using the VDU5 statement to print at the graphics cursor. The MOVE statement in line 10600 moves the graphics cursor to a position sufficiently short of the end of the x axis to allow for the length of the string which is to be inserted. The co-ordinate conversion function is used in the MOVE statements to convert from the range of co-ordinates supplied by the user to the screen co-ordinates.

The operation of PROCnumber: numbering the origin

The condition in line 10620 checks to see if the graph includes both +ve and -ve values along both axes. If so, it only prints the numbers at the positive ends of the x and y axes.

```
10590 DEF PROCnumber :VDU5
10600 MOVE FN£CVX(£LX)-4*LEN(STR$(£LX)),FN£CVY(£Y0)-20
      :PRINT;£LX
10610 MOVEFN£CVX(£X0)-150,FN£CVY(£LY)+28:PRINT;£LY
10620   IF £LX>0AND£SX<0AND£LY>0AND£SY<0THEN ENDPROC
10630 MOVE FN£CVX(£SX),FN£CVY(£Y0)-20:PRINT;£SX
10640 MOVEFN£CVX(£X0)-150,FN£CVY(£SY)+30:PRINT;£SY:VDU4
10650 ENDPROC
```

THE PROCEDURE PROCpoint

PROCpoint marks a single + at the point specified when the procedure is called.

The operation of PROCpoint: the length of the bars

The length of the bars of the + sign is set by the value held in DTA. For most purposes a value of 8 for DTA is suitable. As this routine is used by PROCgraduate, the size of the + is controlled from outside the procedure.

```
10670 DEF PROCpoint(A,B)
10680   MOVEFN£CVX(A)-DTA,FN£CVY(B):DRAWFN£CVX(A)+DTA,
        FN£CVY(B)
10690 MOVEFN£CVX(A),FN£CVY(B)-DTA  :DRAWFN£CVX(A),
        FN£CVY(B)+DTA
10700 ENDPROC
```

THE PROCEDURE PROCgraph

PROCgraph displays a graph consisting of points and it draws axes, graduations and labels for the axes.
    PROCgraph requires an array X() and Y(). X(0) must contain the number of values available within the arrays. X(1), X(2), ... must contain the x co-ordinates and Y(1), Y(2), ... must contain the y co-ordinates.

The operation of PROCgraph

PROCgraph is almost entirely made up from calls to other procedures PROCscale, PROCaxes, PROCgraduate, PROClabel and PROCpoint. The only other type of program lines which it includes define a FOR...NEXT loop to call PROCpoint for each of the points of the graph stored in X() and Y().

```
10000 DEF PROCgraph
10010 PROCscale
10020 PROCaxes
10030 PROCgraduate
10040 PROCnumber
10050 FOR £J=1 TO X(0)
10060   DTA=8 :PROCpoint(X(£J),Y(£J))
10070   NEXT £J
10080 ENDPROC
```

THE PROCEDURE PROCbstln

PROCbstln calculates the straight line which will best represent the points whose co-ordinates are held in the X() and Y() arrays.

The operation of PROCbstln

It is rather meaningless to explain the operation of PROCbstln without also explaining the mathematics behind it - which is beyond the scope of this book. Suffice it to say that lines 10750 and 10760 calculate the mean of the x and y co-ordinates. The sums of the squares of the x and y co-ordinates and their product is then calculated by lines 10770 to 10840. The coefficients M and C are then calculated in line 10850 and 10860 for the equation:

$$Y=MX+C$$

Line 10880 prints up the equation while line 10890 draws the best straight line.

```
10720 DEF PROCbstln
10730 LOCAL C,M,I,XX,YY,MEANX,MEANY,sumX,sumY,sumXY,
      sumYY,sumXX,MINX,MAXX,XY
10740 XX=0 :YY=0:XY=0: sumX=0: sumY=0
10750 FOR I=1 TO X(0) :sumX=sumX+X(I) :sumY=sumY+Y(I)
      :NEXT I
10760 MEANX=sumX/X(0) :MEANY=sumY/X(0)
10770 MINX=X(1):MAXX=MINX:sumXX=0:sumYY=0
      :sumXY=0
10780 FOR I=1 TO X(0)
10790    sumXX=sumXX+X(I)*X(I) :sumYY=sumYY+Y(I)*Y(I)
10800    sumXY=sumXY+X(I)*Y(I)
10810    XX=XX+(X(I)-MEANX)^2 :YY=YY+(Y(I)-MEANY)^2
         :XY=XY+(X(I)-MEANX)*(Y(I)-MEANY)
10820    IF MINX>X(I) THEN MINX=X(I)
10830    IF MAXX<X(I) THEN MAXX=X(I)
10840 NEXT I
10850 M=(X(0)*sumXY-sumX*sumY)/(X(0)*sumXX-sumX*sumX)
10860 C=(sumY*sumXX-sumX*sumXY)/(X(0)*sumXX-sumX*sumX)
10870 @%=&20204 :VDU4
10880 PRINT TAB(10,0);"Y=";M;"*X+";C;TAB(10,1);
      "Cor. coef. = ";XY/SQR(XX*YY)
```

```
10890 MOVE FN£CVX(£SX),FN£CVY(M*£SX+C)
      :DRAW FN£CVX(£LX),FN£CVY(M*£LX+C)
10900 @%=&10 :ENDPROC
```

THE PROCEDURE PROCnamex

PROCnamex names the x axis by printing the required wording along it.

The operation of PROCnamex: positioning the name

The wording is positioned as far to the right as possible using the length of the string as a guide as to where to start printing. The procedure uses VDU5 for printing at the graphics cursor to position each character.

```
10980 DEF PROCnamex(£Hname$)
10990 MOVE FN£CVX(£LX)-32*LEN(£Hname$)-64,
      FN£CVY(£Y0)-52:VDU5:PRINT£Hname$:VDU4
11000 ENDPROC
```

THE PROCEDURE PROCnamey

PROCnamey names the y axis by printing the required wording along it.

The operation of PROCnamey: positioning the name

The procedure does not check whether the name is short enough to fit in the available space and so there may be some odd effects if the name is too long. The procedure uses VDU5 for printing at the graphics cursor to position each character. Hence there is a FOR...NEXT loop set up in line 10930, which steps from 1 to the length of the string. Line 10940 picks off the letters of the name, one by one.

```
10920 DEF PROCnamey(£Vname$):VDU5
10930 FOR £A=1 TO LEN(£Vname$)
10940    MOVE FN£CVX(£X0)-60,FN£CVY(£LY)-£A*32-32
         :PRINTMID$(£Vname$,£A,1)
10950    NEXT £A:VDU4
10960 ENDPROC
```

THE PROCEDURE PROCchr

PROCchr draws a single character at the point specified.
It is called by a line such as:

$$100 \ \text{PROCchr}(X,Y,S\$,AN,SC)$$

where:

X,Y are the co-ordinates of the bottom left-hand corner of the final character when viewed the normal way up.
S$ is the character to be drawn.
SC is how many times larger than normal the character is to be drawn.
AN is the angle at which the character is to be written. 0 corresponds to writing across the screen, while a positive angle measured in radians corresponds to the character being rotated around anticlockwise.

The first numbers representing the x and y co-ordinates must be in screen co-ordinates. If PROCscale has already been called, you can use x in your own co-ordinates, provided you replace x by FN£CVX(x), and similarly for y.

The operation of PROCchr: copying the pixels

The enlarged writing clearly shows the pixels from which the normal character set is made up. This is because the writing is produced by copying the normal character set, together with scaling and rotation as required.

The definitions for all the printable characters are stored in memory as eight numbers per character. These numbers hold the character definitions in precisely the same form as for the programmable characters (see Chapter 4). The call to &FFF1 in line 9050 instructs the operating system to write a copy of the character definition into memory at position M. M is the address of 8 bytes of memory, reserved at the end of the program by line 9040. The FOR ... NEXT loops between lines 9040 and 9080 examine the character definition and write an enlarged pixel wherever it should be lit.

```
9000 DEF PROCchr(X,Y,S$,AN,SC)
9010 LOCAL CO1,CO2,SI1,SI2,LX,LY,RX,RY,XX,YY
9020 CO1=COS(AN):SI1=-SIN(AN)
9030 CO2=COS(PI/2-AN):SI2=SIN(AN+PI/2)
9040 £F=£F+1:IF £F=1 THEN DIM M 8 ELSE £F=2
9050 A%=10:X%=M MOD256:Y%=M DIV256:?M=ASC(S$):CALL(&FFF1)
9060 FOR XX=0TO7 :FOR YY=0TO7
9070   IF ?(M+8-YY) AND 2^(7-XX) THEN PROCpixel
9080   NEXT YY,XX
9090 ENDPROC
9100 DEF PROCpixel
9110 LX=XX-.5:RX=XX+.5:LY=YY-.5:RY=YY+.5
9120 MOVE X+SC*(LX*CO1+LY*SI1),Y+SC*(LY*SI2+LX*CO2)
9130 MOVE X+SC*(RX*CO1+LY*SI1),Y+SC*(LY*SI2+RX*CO2)
9140 PLOT 85,X+SC*(LX*CO1+RY*SI1),Y+SC*(RY*SI2+LX*CO2)
9150 PLOT 85,X+SC*(RX*CO1+RY*SI1),Y+SC*(RY*SI2+RX*CO2)
9160 ENDPROC
```

THE PROCEDURE PROCmessage

PROCmessage writes a message on the screen.
   It is called by a line such as:

        PROCmessage(X,Y,S$,AN,SC)

where:

X,Y are the co-ordinates of the bottom left-hand corner of the first character when viewed the normal way up.
S$ is the message to be drawn.
AN is the angle at which the message is to be written. It is slightly unusual in that 0 corresponds to writing straight up the screen, while a positive angle measured in radians corresponds to the message being rotated around anticlockwise.
SC is how many times larger than normal the character is to be drawn.

The operation of PROCmessage: printing the characters

Lines 9220 and 9230 calculate the position at which the character is to be drawn. A call to PROCchr in line 9240 then displays the next character.

```
9180 DEFPROCmessage(X,Y,S$,AN,SC)
9190 LOCAL I,XP,YP
9200 AN=AN+PI/2
9210 FOR I=1 TO LEN(S$)
9220    XP=SC*(COS(AN)*8*(I-1))
9230    YP=SC*(SIN(AN)*8*(I-1))
9240    PROCchr(X+XP,Y+YP,MID$(S$,I,1),AN,SC)
9250    NEXT I
9260 ENDPROC
```

THE PROCEDURE PROCcurve

PROCcurve prints a message on the screen round the arc of a circle.
   It is called by a line such as:

PROCcurve(X,Y,R,SA,FA,S$,SC)

where:

X,Y are the co-ordinates of the bottom left-hand corner of the final character when viewed normal way up.
R   is the radius of the circle round which the writing is to appear.
SA is the angle round the circle at which writing is to begin. This is slightly unusual in that 0 corresponds to a position straight above the centre of the circle, while a positive angle measured in radians corresponds to the starting position rotating around anticlockwise.
FA is the angle round the circle at which writing is to finish.
S$ is the message to be drawn.
SC is how many times larger than normal the character is to be drawn.

The operation of PROCcurve

Lines 9320 and 9330 calculate the position for the next character to be drawn, while a call to PROCchr in line 9340 draws it on the screen.

```
9280 DEFPROCcurve(X,Y,R,SA,FA,S$,SC)
9290 LOCAL I,XP,YP
9300 SA=SA+PI/2:FA=FA+PI/2
9310 FOR I=1 TO LEN(S$)
9320   XP=X+R*COS(SA-(SA-FA)*(I-1)/(LEN(S$)+1))
9330   YP=Y+R*SIN(SA-(SA-FA)*(I-1)/(LEN(S$)+1))
9340   PROCchr(XP,YP,MID$(S$,I,1),SA-(SA-FA)*(I-1)/
       (LEN(S$)+1)-PI/2,SC)
9350   NEXT I
9360 ENDPROC
```

THE PROCEDURE PROChisto

PROChisto draws bars of a histogram of height equal to the values held in the Y() array when converted to screen co-ordinates. So PROCscale has to be called before PROChisto.

The operation of PROChisto: the bar position

The values held in the X() array are taken as the co-ordinates of the right-hand side of the bars. The width of the bars is made equal to the step size along the x axis which is held in the variable £ST, after PROCscale has been called. Thus the x co-ordinates to the left and right of the bars and the y co-ordinate of the top and bottom of the bars are worked out in lines 12040 to 12060. Then lines 12100 and 12110 draw up the bars. The colour for each bar is alternately 1 and 2 as set by line 12030.

```
12000 DEF PROChisto
12010 £C=1
12020 FOR £A=1 TO X(0)-1
12030   GCOL0,£C :£C=£C+1 :IF £C>2 THEN £C=1
12040   £XL=FN£CVX(X(£A)-£IN) :£XR=FN£CVX(X(£A))
12050   £YH=FN£CVY(Y(£A))
```

```
12060    £YB=FN£CVY(0)
12070    MOVE £XL,£YB :MOVE £XL,£YH
12080    PLOT 85,£XR,£YB :PLOT 85,£XR,£YH
12090    GCOL 0,3
12100    MOVE £XL,£YB :DRAW £XR,£YB
12110    DRAW £XR,£YH :DRAW £XL,£YH :DRAW £XL,£YB
12120    NEXT £A
12130  ENDPROC
```

THE PROCEDURE PROC3Dhisto

PROC3Dhisto draws up solid-looking bars for a histogram. This is
particularly useful when two histograms need to be superimposed,
one in front of the other.

The operation of PROC3Dhisto

The principle is very similar to that for PROChisto in the use of
the X() array to hold the right hand co-ordinate of the bars and
the Y() array to hold the bar heights. The front of the bar is
plotted by lines 12200 and 12210, as two triangles to give a solid
block of colour; the side is produced by lines 12230 and 12240;
and the top is filled in by lines 12260 and 12270. The set of
DRAW statements in lines 12290 to 12340 then mark out the
edges of the blocks to make the picture more distinct.

```
12150 DEF PROC3Dhisto(C)
12160 FOR £A=1 TO X(0)-1
12170    £XL=FN£CVX(X(£A)-£IN) :£XR=FN£CVX(X(£A))
12180    £YB=FN£CVY(0) :£YH=FN£CVY(Y(£A))
12190    GCOL 0,C
12200    MOVE £XL,£YB :MOVE £XL,£YH
12210    PLOT 85,£XR,£YB :PLOT 85,£XR,£YH
12220    GCOL 0,3-C
12230    PLOT 85,£XR+64,£YB+32
12240    PLOT 85,£XR+64,£YH+32
12250    MOVE £XR,£YH
12260    PLOT 85,£XL+64,£YH+32
12270    PLOT 85,£XL,£YH
12280    GCOL 0,3
12290    MOVE £XL,£YH:DRAW £XL+64,£YH+32
```

```
12300    DRAW £XR+64,£YH+32
12310    DRAW £XR,£YH:DRAW £XL,£YH
12320    DRAW £XL,£YB:DRAW £XR,£YB
12330    DRAW £XR,£YH:DRAW £XR+64,£YH+32
12340    DRAW £XR+64,£YB+32:DRAW£XR,£YB
12350    NEXT £A
12360 ENDPROC
```

THE PROCEDURE PROCpie

PROCpie draws up a pie chart from data stored in the arrays £S() and £N$(). PROCpie is quite different from the rest and so we chose different array names to help emphasize this point.

The operation of PROCpie

The relative size of each sector of the pie-chart is held in £S() while the total sum of these relative sizes is held in T. The first part of the procedure steps through all the sectors (the FOR...NEXT loop between lines 13030 and 13090). It calls on the sub-procedure PROCsector (see later) to draw each sector while supplying this sub-procedure with the starting and ending fraction of the whole that the sector should occupy.

Only three colours are used for the pie chart, two being used for alternate sectors with the last sector always being in the third colour. This ensures that even for an even number of sectors, no two sectors have the same colour (see lines 13050 and 13060.)

```
13000 DEF PROCpie(R%,X%,Y%,T)
13010 LOCAL L%,S,W
13020 W=0:S=0:C%=0
13030 FOR L%=1 TO £NS
13040    W=W+£S(L%)
13050    C%=C%+1:IFC%>2THENC%=1
13060    IFL%=£NS THENC%=3
13070    PROCsector(C%,S/T,W/T,R%,X%,Y%)
13080    S=W
13090    NEXTL%
13100 PROClabel(R%,X%,Y%,T)
13110 ENDPROC
```

THE PROCEDURE PROCsector

PROCsector is a subsidiary part of PROCpie and draws an individual sector.

The operation of PROCsector

PROCsector sets the colour for the sector in line 13150. Then it does an initial MOVE to the outside radius at the start of the sector. Line 13160 calculates this initial position by adding the projection of the radius in first the x and then the y direction to the co-ordinates for the centre. This first MOVE, followed by a second one to the centre of the pie chart in line 13180, is necessary as extensive use is made of the triangular form of the PLOT statement. This occurs in line 13190 which is now within a FOR...NEXT loop which moves the x and y co-ordinates of the PLOT85 statement in line 13190 round the circumference of the pie chart. This results in many calls to the triangular fill form of the PLOT statement and causes the sector to be filled in the chosen colour.

```
13130 DEF PROCsector(C%,S,F,R%,X%,Y%)
13140 LOCAL L
13150 GCOL0,C%
13160 MOVE COS(2*PI*S)*R%+X%,SIN(2*PI*S)*R%+Y%
13170 FOR L= 2*PI*S TO 2*PI*F STEP 0.1
13180   MOVE X%,Y%
13190   PLOT 85,COS(L)*R%+X%,SIN(L)*R%+Y%
13200   NEXTL
13210 PLOT85,COS(2*PI*F)*R%+X%,SIN(2*PI*F)*R%+Y%
13220 ENDPROC
```

THE PROCEDURE PROClabel

PROClabel is solely for labelling pie-charts. It is for this reason that we have chosen it to use the same variation of arrays £S() and £N$() as for PROCpie.

The operation of PROClabel

PROClabel positions each label to start or end at a position just outside the pie chart and off the centre of the particular sector referred to. This means that the main calculation, which occurs in line 13290, has to calculate the projection of a length slightly longer than the radius of the pie-chart. It then adds this to the co-ordinates of the centre of the pie-chart to find the position for the label. The radial position chosen for the label corresponds to the centre of that particular sector, as determined in line 13270. Here B represents the fraction of the pie-chart occupied by previous sectors, and is updated in line 13310 after each label has been printed.

Since each label is printed by a normal PRINT statement, it is necessary to make sure that for labels on the left of the pie-chart that the printing starts at a position displaced to the left according to the length of the label. This offset leftwards is calculated in line 13280.

```
13240 DEF PROClabel(R%,X%,Y%,T)
13250 VDU5:B=0:R%=R%+64
13260 FOR A=1 TO £NS
13270   OX=0:H=(B+£S(A)/2)*2*PI/T
13280   IFH<PI*1.5 ANDH>PI*.5 THENOX=-(LEN(£N$(A)))*32)
13290   MOVE COS(H)*R%+X%+OX,SIN(H)*R%+Y%
13300   PRINT£N$(A)
13310   B=B+£S(A)
13320   NEXTA
13330 VDU4
13340 ENDPROC
```

THE TELETEXT PROCEDURE PROCplot

Teletext graphics is so much more crude than the other graphics modes that we decided to plot individual points on the screen as single dots rather than as the + signs used in the ordinary graphics procedures. This point plotting is achieved by a PROCplot which is unique to Teletext. It is in place of PROCpoint for the normal graphics modes. There is still the equivalent of PROCpoint for drawing a small + sign as this was required when graduating the axes (see later). If you should wish to plot a graph with a + sign to represent each point then use PROCpoint in line 10060.

```
11200 DEFPROCplot(X,Y)
11210 IF X>73 OR X<0 THEN ENDPROC
11220 IF Y>74 OR Y<0 THEN ENDPROC
11230 LOCAL A%,C%
11240 PRINT TAB(X DIV 2,24-Y DIV 3);
11250 C%=(X AND1)+(Y MOD3)*2
11260 C%=VAL(MID$("166404080102",C%*2+1,2))
11270 A%=135
11280 VDU (USR &FFF4 AND &FF00) DIV 256 OR C% OR 128
11290 ENDPROC
```

THE TELETEXT PROCEDURE PROCdraw

This procedure is unique to Teletext, and is required to do the equivalent of the MOVE and DRAW statements of ordinary graphics. It relies on Pythagoras's theorem to work a way between the two points whose co-ordinates are given in the procedure call.

```
11310 DEFPROCdraw(X1,Y1,X2,Y2)
11320 PROCplot(X1,Y1) :PROCplot(X2,Y2)
11330 LOCAL X,Y,L,A
11340 X=(X2-X1) :Y=(Y2-Y1)
11350 L=SQR((X1-X2)^2+(Y1-Y2)^2)
11360 FOR A=1 TO L
11370    IF L<>0 THEN PROCplot(X1+A*X/L,Y1+A*Y/L)
11380    NEXT A
11390 ENDPROC
```

THE TELETEXT PROCEDURE PROCclg

This procedure is unique to Teletext. Block graphics may only be displayed after certain control codes to the left of any line. This procedure writes these control codes all the way down the left-hand side of screen.

```
11050 DEFPROCclg(C,G)
11060 VDU 28,0,24,39,0,23,0,10,32;0;0;0;
11070 LOCAL CH,GH,Y
11080 CH=128+C : CLS
11090 IF C<1 OR C>7 THEN CH=132
11100 GH=144+G
11110 IF G<1 OR G>7 THEN GH=156
11120 FOR Y=0 TO 24
11130   PRINT TAB(0,Y);
11140   VDU CH,157,GH
11150   NEXT Y
11160 VDU 28,3,24,39,0
11170 PRINT TAB(0,0);
11180 ENDPROC
```

THE TELETEXT PROCEDURE PROCgraph

The Teletext version of this procedure is identical to the ordinary version, except that a call to PROCplot in line 1060 replaces the call to PROCpoint.

```
10000 DEF PROCgraph
10010 PROCscale
10020 PROCaxes
10030 PROCgraduate
10040 PROCnumber
10050 FOR £J=1 TO X(0)
10060   PROCplot(FN£CVX(X(£J)),FN£CVY(Y(£J)))
10070   NEXT £J
10080 ENDPROC
```

THE TELETEXT PROCEDURE PROCscale

The Teletext version of PROCscale is very similar to the ordinary version. The differences are in lines 10240 and 10250 which define the conversion function from numbers supplied by the user's program to screen co-ordinates.

THE TELETEXT PROCEDURE PROCaxes

The Teletext version of PROCaxes is different from the ordinary version because it involves writing on the screen. In place of the MOVE and DRAW statements of the normal graphics procedures, it calls upon a specially written PROCdraw procedure in lines 10460 and 10470.

```
10460  PROCdraw(FN£CVX(£SX),FN£CVY(£YØ),FN£CVX(£LX),
       FN£CVY(£YØ))
10470  PROCdraw(FN£CVX(£XØ),FN£CVY(£SY),FN£CVX(£XØ),
       FN£CVY(£LY))
```

THE TELETEXT PROCEDURE PROCgraduate

The Teletext version of PROCgraduate is identical to the ordinary version. The PROCpoint which it calls upon in line 10530 and 10560 must, however, be the special Teletext one.

```
10530    £CBX%=£CBX%+1 :PROCpoint(x,£YØ) :NEXT x
         ...
10560    £CBY%=£CBY%+1 :PROCpoint(£XØ,y) :NEXT y
```

THE TELETEXT PROCEDURE PROCnumber

Since PROCnumber writes on the Teletext screen, it is completely different from the ordinary version. The Teletext screen is set up with the assumption that the whole screen will contain only graphics. To write text at a particular position, PROCplot (in line 10600 and elsewhere) positions where to write. This procedure also writes a single graphics dot on the screen which is erased by printing code 127 to delete the last character written. Code 134, in Teletext, switches on cyan coloured writing. Next comes whatever number is required for the axes, followed by code 147 to turn the graphics back on.

Each code to turn from graphics to normal writing or from normal writing to graphics occupies one character position on the screen. As a result it is impossible to write long numbers against the y axis without sometimes overwriting part of the axis itself.

This is yet another manifestation of the insuperable problems of the poor resolution which is available with Teletext.

```
10590 DEF PROCnumber
10600 PROCplot(FN£CVX(£LX)-LEN(STR$(£LX)),FN£CVY(£Y0)-3)
      :PRINTCHR$127;CHR$134;£LX;CHR$147;
10610 PROCplot(FN£CVX(£X0)-7,FN£CVY(£LY)+4):
      PRINTCHR$127;CHR$134;£LY;CHR$147;
10620 IF £LX>0AND£SX<0AND£LY>0AND£SY<0 THEN ENDPROC
10630 PROCplot(FN£CVX(£SX)-7,FN£CVY(£Y0)-3):
      PRINTCHR$127;CHR$134;£SX;CHR$147;
10640 PROCplot(FN£CVX(£X0)-7,FN£CVY(£SY)):
      PRINTCHR$127;CHR$134;£SY;CHR$147;
10650 ENDPROC
```

THE TELETEXT PROCEDURE PROCpoint

The Teletext version of PROCpoint is different from the ordinary version. It makes considerable use of the Teletext procedure PROCdraw (see later), referred to in lines 10680 and 10690, which draws a line between two points.

```
10670 DEF PROCpoint(A,B)
10680 PROCdraw(FN£CVX(A)-DTA,FN£CVY(B),FN£CVX(A)+DTA,
      FN£CVY(B))
10690 PROCdraw(FN£CVX(A),FN£CVY(B)-DTA,FN£CVX(A),
      FN£CVY(B)+DTA)
10700 ENDPROC
```

THE TELETEXT PROCEDURE PROCbstln

The Teletext version of PROCbstln is identical to the ordinary version except for the line 10910 which prints on the screen and line 10920 which calls on PROCdraw to draw the best straight line.

```
10910 PRINT TAB(9,0);CHR$135;"Y=";M;"*X+";C;CHR$147;TAB
      (9,1);CHR$135;"Cor. coef. = ";XY/SQR(XX*YY);CHR$147
10920 PROCdraw(FN£CVX(£SX),FN£CVY(M*£SX+C),FN£CVX(£LX),
      FN£CVY(M*£LX+C))
```

THE TELETEXT PROCEDURE PROCnamey

The Teletext version of PROCnamey is different from the ordinary version. It writes the name of the y axis one character at a time in a vertical column. PROCplot positions the writing. This also writes a single graphics point, which is rubbed out by printing character code 127, followed by code 135 for white writing, followed in turn by the single letter required. The graphics is then turned back again for the rest of the line with code 147 for yellow graphics.

```
10950 DEF PROCnamey(£Vname$)
10960 FOR £A=1 TO LEN(£Vname$)
10970   PROCplot(FN£CVX(£XØ)-8,FN£CVY(£LY)-£A*3+3):PRINT
        CHR$127;CHR$135;MID$(£Vname$,£A,1);CHR$147;
10980   NEXT £A
```

THE TELETEXT PROCEDURE PROCnamex

The Teletext version of PROCnamex is different from the ordinary version. It is also simpler in that the whole name is written on one line. This means that the process can be achieved in the one line 11210 by first calling on PROCplot to get the position to start printing. The graphics spot so produced is then rubbed out using code 127, followed by code 135 for white writing. The name is then merely printed next using a PRINT statement. This is followed by code 147 to turn yellow graphics back on again. The position at which to begin the writing is calculated by subtracting the length of the string to be written from the co-ordinates of the end of the axis. Before doing this subtraction in line 11020, the length of the string is scaled to allow for the two graphics spots which occur in the length occupied by one letter.

```
11010 DEF PROCnamex(£Hname$)
11020 PROCplot(FN£CVX(£LX)-2*LEN(£Hname$)-3,
      FN£CVY(£YØ)-6):VDU127,135:PRINT£Hname$;CHR$147;
11030 ENDPROC
```

Appendix 3   The ASCII codes

Decimal Values of ASCII Characters

	Units 0	1	2	3	4	5	6	7	8	9
0		SOH	STX	ETX	EOT	ENQ	ACK	BEL	BS	HT
10	LF	VT	FF	CR	SO	SI	DLE	DC1	DC2	DC3
20	DC4	NAK	SYN	ETB	CAN	EM	SUB	ESC	FS	GS
30	RS	US	SP	!	"	#	$	%	&	'
40	(	)	*	+	,	-	.	/	0	1
50	2	3	4	5	6	7	8	9	:	;
60	<	=	>	?	@	A	B	C	D	E
70	F	G	H	I	J	K	L	M	N	O
80	P	Q	R	S	T	U	V	W	X	Y
90	Z	[	\	]	^	_	`	a	b	c
100	d	e	f	g	h	i	j	k	l	m
110	n	o	p	q	r	s	t	u	v	w
120	x	y	z	{	|	}	~			

Index

The Authors

Neil Cryer obtained his PhD in physics at the University of Exeter in 1961, and is now a lecturer at Chelsea College, University of London where he teaches physics and microprocessor applications. He is a joint founder of the West London Personal Computer Club and a committee member of the Association of London Computer Clubs. He is a regular contributor of articles and reviews in computing magazines.

Pat Cryer obtained her BSc in physics and mathematics at the University of Exeter and her PhD in educational studies at the University of Surrey. She is active in the education and training of adults in aspects of teaching and learning. In this connection she has been a visiting lecturer at the University of Malaya and at Makerere University, Uganda and she is an honorary research fellow in the Institute of Educational Development at the University of Surrey. Her specialism is education and training through printed materials. She has undertaken various consultancies on training materials, including one to a major international computing company, and she acts as co-ordinator and editor for the Society for Research into Higher Education working group to produce materials to support the training of university lecturers.

Andrew Cryer has had articles published in Acorn User. He is currently in the sixth form at Burlington Danes School, Hammersmith, studying computing, physics and mathematics.